Praise for
The Joy of Creative Discovery

Looking for inspirational gems and practical tools to catapult you into the amazing next chapter of your life? You'll love Pasha Hogan's ***The Joy of Creative Discovery***. More than a workbook, it's a funbook, rich in creativity and spirituality. Pasha is a wise guide, ready to accompany you on a journey that will shake up your life in the best way possible!

~ **Kris Carr, *New York Times* best-selling author**

Have you experienced times when creative moments occur unexpectedly and unbidden, as if from another dimension, often with a sense of joy or ecstasy? What if we could have these experiences at will? This ability lies within the reach of nearly everyone, as Pasha Hogan shows in ***The Joy of Creative Discovery.*** Practical, down to earth, and immensely enjoyable, this book is a journey to the visionary, innovative side that is part of our human endowment.

~ **Larry Dossey, MD, author of One Mind: *How Our Individual Mind Is Part of a Greater Consciousness* and *Why It Matters***

Pasha has put together an amazing workbook for getting your "beginner's mind" working in service of your creativity. Put perfectionism aside and play in the joyful world of inner transformation. It's deeply spiritual and, at the same time, such fun!

~ **Parvati Markus, author of *Love Everyone***

In this step-by-step workbook, Pasha holds our hands and helps us through a journey to rediscover the innocence, peace, joy, and beauty that have been within us all along. The practices can transform one's life.

~ GARY DENG, MD, PhD, Medical Director, Integrative Medicine Memorial Sloan Kettering Cancer Center

Get ready to open to the exciting creative gifts awaiting you in your life! Pasha Hogan's ***The Joy of Creative Discovery*** is so engaging, so warm and insightful, that you feel like Pasha is sitting with you over a cup of tea, encouraging you forward in your quest for your own gifts, self-love, and creative expression. Pasha's life path as an inspiring teacher, wise therapist, and deep soul traveler informs her marvelous book. Her exercises call you to free yourself from the voices that hold you back, and her teachings exude the authenticity, wisdom, and light of one who has walked a profound life path, and generously shares the gold she's discovered. Buy this marvelous book, and share in Pasha's bounty.

~ CHRISTINE WARREN, author of *Navigating Change: Conscious Endings, Visionary Beginnings*

In 2013, Pasha Hogan wrote a deeply personal book —***Third Time Lucky***—describing her descent into the cauldron of cancer and the way that this catapulted her into greater mystery and a deeper connection to life itself. ***The Joy of Creative Discovery*** was born from this book, providing tools that help the reader sweep away ghosts of the past and doubts and judgements that block the creative process. This workbook is shockingly comprehensive, with practices spanning from establishing a nourishing morning ritual, creating an altar, and witnessing and energizing the heart, to practices in forgiveness, gratitude, not knowing, learning to rest, and self-compassion.

Pasha writes directly from her own experience in a profoundly vulnerable way, hiding nothing and modeling the very process that she so beautifully articulates. Her voice is so authentic that you feel like you are sitting in her living room and sharing a cup of tea, as she speaks from the wisdom of her heart. She makes the complex process of connecting to one's inner life beautifully accessible to all.

~ **JAN BIRCHFIELD, PhD, author of *Silent Leaders***

Pasha Hogan has created a sanctuary, a sacred garden where we may be inspired, nurtured, and replenished. The practices gleaned from ancient and contemporary wisdom plant seeds in the soil of our hearts. With courage, curiosity, patience, and perseverance these seeds grow and blossom into our own beloved selves.

The Joy of Creative Discovery is more than a book. It is a process of transformation. Pasha asks, "What needs tending to in your heart?" As a gardener tends to the soil, we are invited to feel our feelings like roots spreading down deep into the moist, dark soil and our stems rising up towards the light of the sun, never knowing what fruits we will bear.

~ **Celeste Yacoboni**, author of *How Do You Pray?*

I have personally experienced Pasha Hogan's life-giving retreats and workshops. And so, I know that this rich and beautiful ***Joy of Creative Discovery*** workbook will be a blessing to all who want to begin or to continue on a path of healing, forgiveness, wholeness, and creativity. Pasha has the special gift of unconditional love for all of us who have experienced her workshops, and this love shines through this new workbook. The activities are simple yet profound and move us into the sacred space of the heart. Treat yourself to life abundant and walk this path with Pasha.

~ **Lyn Holley Doucet**, author of *Water from Stones: An Inner Journey, Healing Troubled Hearts, When Wisdom Speaks,* and *Light on a River's Turning*

In this historical time of great challenge and change, it is most important that each of us creates personal practices that support our individual well-being and resiliency. In this workbook, Pasha Hogan becomes our loving and potent guide, empowering us all to find our most authentic expression of self and to live that with boldness and joy. In Pasha's practices, we are given gentle, ancient wisdom in a contemporary, accessible form that all of us can utilize for dynamic self-care. The consciousness and values that unfold for each individual create a personal foundation for each of us to align with as we choose further contribution to our communities and the collective. I highly recommend Pasha's powerful hands-on "play" book that guides us to create a personal, delightful, valuable, and substantial path.

~ **Valerie Valentine, art therapist and illustrator of the Dreaming of Peace collection**

Pasha Hogan invites creative exploration to reconnect with your authenticity. As an exemplar of her own journey, she graciously lights the way for courageous self-discovery.

~ **Kim Lincoln, author of *Holy Here Wholy You, Discovering Your Authentic Self***

In her compassionate, practical, and visionary book, Pasha invites us to whole-heartedly commit to our creative selves—the "healing artist" within—who carries our gifts and most essential offerings. She encourages each of us to move beyond our comfort zone and discover the edges of our known world, so that we can live the creative life we have always dreamed of. Her elegant and accessible practices, meditations, and reflections serve as a bridge between our inner "wishful thinking" and actualization, and they illuminate a path to a creative life of fulfillment, joy, and self-love. Pasha heart-fully invites us to see, honor, and express our unique and creative spark that is our natural birthright and essence. ***The Joy of Creative Discovery*** is a delightful and invaluable tool for anyone on the creative path—which is ALL of us.

~ LAURA WEAVER, author of *Luminous*

The Joy of Creative Discovery

PRACTICES TO RECLAIM YOUR PURPOSE AND PASSION

Pasha Hogan

For Travis, 4/28/18.
Bright Beautiful Blessings to you as you continue to discover your own magnificence + all that you bring!
Love Pasha

Emerald Flame
Publishing

For more information contact:
info@emeraldflamepublishing.com

978-0-9885511-3-8 (paperback)
978-0-9885511-4-5 (eBook)

Printed in the U.S.A.

Book design by DesignForBooks.com
Cover and interior illustrations by Michael Rohani

Disclaimer

In the examples in this book regarding the author's clients, names have been changed to respect confidentiality. The author of this book does not dispense medical or clinical psychotherapeutic advice or prescribe the use of any techniques as a form of treatment for a physical, emotional, or medical problem. The intent of the author is only to offer information of a general nature to help readers in their quest for personal, emotional and spiritual growth. In the event you use any of the information in this book for yourself, the author and the publisher assume no responsibility for your actions.

This book is dedicated to
my sister, Eileen Hogan Grant,
for showing up for me in a heartbeat
loving my laugh and making me laugh
the road trips
car karaoke
believing in me
supporting my dreams
sharing your wisdom
and mostly, because you are my
magnificent sister and always will be
I love you.

Dragonfly symbolizes the transcendence of self-created illusions.

Are you ready?

CONTENTS

Introduction

> *We are all inventors, each sailing out on a voyage of discovery, guided each by a private chart, of which there is no duplicate. The world is all gates, all opportunities.*
>
> ~ Ralph Waldo Emerson

I will let you in on a secret: you don't have to know.

As adults we think we have to know so much. That is the thinking that keeps us stuck in our comfort zones, playing it small, playing it safe, and feeling like we are not good enough.

Children can teach us a lot. They are not dismayed by what they don't know. Instead, they are joyous with each new discovery.

This workbook invites you to awaken the innocence of the child that lives within you—your original innocence. It also invites you to step out of your own comfort zone and enter your discovery zone, full of childlike curiosity and wonder. Don't worry, you are not alone on this adventure!

To be like a child is to be close to God. If, for any reason at all, that word does not resonate with you, please change it to whatever word or phrase translates to an all-encompassing Love that never judges, knows you by name, and is longing for you to remember that you are here for a purpose and have a unique contribution to share with the world.

There is nothing frivolous about connecting with your innocence. It takes enormous courage and maturity. Your childlike self holds secrets, all kinds of secrets, which have long been forgotten. Maybe even ninety-nine secrets. Some may be uncomfortable, others so delightful that you want to do a little dance in front of your living room mirror when no one is watching. Hopefully, by the end of this book, you won't care if anyone is watching or not.

Cultivating an attitude of childlike innocence will free you to grow into the human being you are destined to be—an adult who stays curious and lives with purpose and passion. I don't know what that looks like for you. It looks different for everyone, but it *feels* the same for all of us.

Imagine how you could feel if you didn't feel dismayed or overwhelmed by what you didn't know. Not knowing is an invitation to try on new ideas, to lighten up, to play, to make new choices, and to create new practices.

When I finished my first book, *Third Time Lucky: A Creative Recovery*, I was sure that this workbook, its companion and sister, would follow within the year—so much so that I included a portion of the first chapter in the afterword. That was over three years ago.

I thought I knew how long it would take. Well, guess what? *I didn't know*!

I got catapulted out of my own comfort zone time and time again while writing this, and few things went the way I thought they would or should.

At times it was frustrating. Often I felt impatient with myself and the process, putting the manuscript down for days, weeks, months. But I never gave up believing in its completion.

Why? Because for over ten years I saw and heard about the benefits people experienced by attending my *Creative Discovery* workshops and engaging in many of the practices in these pages. All kinds of people: mostly people who were going through huge transitions and were seeking a greater purpose and meaning in their life; people who declared they were not creative and then marveled at what was inside of them, just waiting for a chance to be expressed; people from all walks of life, who were willing not to know, who brought an attitude of humility to the table, and later feasted on the fruits of their efforts. Amazing people, just like you.

This book was born from those workshops and comes to you as a series of practices. Anyone can practice. You don't have to be good, talented, or special to practice. In fact, all you need to do is show up, be willing to be a beginner every day, put some time and effort into the process, and see what happens. The attitude and energy behind *how* you approach each practice is far more important than *what* you think you are going to get out of it.

Practice simply means *noticing*. Few of us are able to learn a foreign language unless we begin with the basics and take it slow. Learning, or unlearning, can be a laborious and tedious process for the adult who is used to "getting it right," looking like they know what is going on, and keeping it together.

You may get frustrated or feel overwhelmed at times. No big deal! We all do. It's normal. Just put it down for a while and come back to it later. If you want to start a different practice in the book, skip around or go back to an earlier one, please do. There is no way you can fail or get it wrong. Remember, there is no particular way anything is supposed to look.

When you try out the practices in this book, think *kindergarten*! I encourage you to participate with an enthusiastic, open heart and let yourself be surprised.

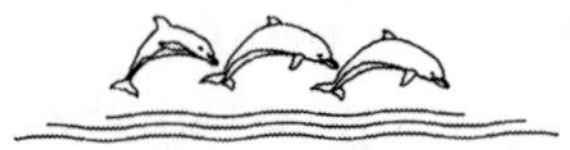

Practice

Being Inspired

Work honestly. Meditate every day. Meet people without fear, and play.

~ Baba Hari Dass

You may want to write out the quote opposite in crayon or print it out in a fun font. Put it someplace you'll see before you leave home every day. It's on the inside of my front door.

Reasons to Embark on the Joy and Practice of Creative Discovery

Here are a few statements I often hear, to give you an idea and perhaps even get you started on your own list.

1. Why not?
2. I want more happiness in my life.
3. I want a job that suits my personality.
4. There has to be more to life than this.
5. I want to be seen.
6. Everything is the way it is "supposed to be," and I still feel like something is missing.
7. Nothing is the way it is "supposed" to be.
8. I feel like a phony.
9. Life feels too hard.

Psst! This may be the one list you want to give yourself permission to keep adding to for the rest of your life.

Helpful Guidelines

- ★ Love Yourself
- ★ Be Curious
- ★ Be Kind
- ★ Be Patient
- ★ Be Respectful
- ★ Have Fun

You are worthy of this effort.
Go for it. Have fun. You can't fail. I promise. I love you.
Just practice and breathe.

With tremendous love and respect,

Pasha
Santa Fe, New Mexico
September 2017

1

The Practice of Beginning

Getting Started: Stepping into the Unknown

Before starting a new creative project, I begin to notice how much I need to do the dishes, vacuum, file my nails, redecorate the house, call my mother, catch up on all my emails, and plan dinner. Every time! It doesn't matter that I know this—I still do it. Everybody does. You are not alone in your procrastination.

Why do we do this? I believe we put off these creative play times, work times, and fun times because we know, deep inside, that it will change us in some way. When we face a blank page, canvas, or closed book, we do not know what will rise up inside of ourselves, and most of us find that a little scary. The fear of nothing rising up to meet us scares us too—it may even be unconscious; it doesn't matter. Though I now know how transformative it will be once I start, a part of me is still afraid of what might be revealed, afraid that what I produce might not be good enough.

Guess what? It won't ever be good enough as long as you believe *you* are not enough. As long as you believe you are not enough, no thing or no one will ever be enough, either. All you need right now is to understand that the following exercises are not about the product. They are about the process, *your process.* They are about how you feel while you are doing them. And later, when you step back and look at the results for the very first time, it will be about the enduring relationship you enter into with both the process and the result.

The next time you notice yourself booking a dentist appointment instead of gathering images for your collage, writing in your journal, or taking a long, hot bubble bath, stop and ask yourself, very kindly and very gently, "What is this?" Most likely, it is you putting off the very thing that you want most. So be gentle and be firm. It takes courage to start, and it takes courage to change. This is your time to be seen and heard.

Heads up! Your inner critic, judge, or commentator will try to stop you. Using practices and creative exercises will help unleash that creative spirit of yours, helping you to let go of perfectionism and become more playful.

The idea of playing has sometimes put the fear of God in me. Play? What's that? I don't have time to play. But remember, it is playing, not performing. Play is how we discover new knowledge. Loosen up *how* you think play is supposed to look, and let play just *happen.*

To live a creative life, we must lose our fear of being wrong.

~ Joseph Chilton Pearce

Handling the Inner Critic

Starting any new relationship can be daunting, especially one with ourselves. It's often tempting to slip into habitual, negative self-talk, which, after all, only serves the purpose of keeping you stuck. *What if it doesn't work? What if I am no good? What if I am not creative?* Heads up, folks: almost every single person I have worked with has immediately announced to me, off the bat, that they are not creative—including myself.

What if "just for today," you could suspend the negative self-talk and try something new?

A few years back, while struggling to write *Third Time Lucky*, I put together these "Just for Today" principles. They have become a guide for my day-to-day life. Since then, I have shared them with countless others who have found them to be helpful companions on their journeys.

Noticing a habit, thought, or feeling doesn't always require us to analyze it, figure it out, or judge it. Whenever my inner critic intrudes, I use one, some, or all of these principles (depending on how loud the negative self-talk is) to keep me grounded in the moment and to help me remember it's only my critic talking—it's not me! The following "Just for Today" principles can accompany you on your journey, too.

Just for Today . . .

I am breathing in warmth and kindness toward myself

I am excessively gentle with myself

I am greeting my reflection with a softened gaze

I am giving myself permission to make beautiful mistakes

I am my own compassionate witness

Prefacing each affirmation with "just for today" brings it right into the *now,* and that is where our power is. "Just for today" is manageable and possible; very often "always" and "forever" are not. I suggest you write these down on postcards and put them in places you will see, to remind yourself to silence the negative self-talk. My "Just for Today" cards have been taped to my bathroom mirror, desk, and refrigerator over the years, and there is one by my side as I write this now.

Let's have a closer look at each.

I am breathing in warmth and kindness toward myself.

Right now, just stop and imagine your next breath is full of warmth and kindness toward yourself. Feel the warmth and kindness entering through your nose and immediately spreading across your chest, into your heart, and down into your belly, filling your whole body with tenderness toward yourself. Imagine that each breath is life rushing toward you, each breath a second chance. Imagine each exhale is you going toward life.

I am excessively gentle with myself.

Okay, I don't mean being kind of nice or not being too mean or hard on yourself. I mean being "excessively" gentle. Most people tell me they have no idea what being gentle with themselves *looks* like, let alone *being* excessively gentle. You can start by imagining how you would treat your five-year-old self. What does she need in this moment? A hug, smile, warm bubble bath, flowers, cup of hot chocolate? Something that lets her know you are here for her. Keep it simple and real. Enter where you are, without putting pressure on yourself. The excessive part can come by consciously tending to yourself with softness and kindness the moment you notice your harsh, critical voice creeping in. You can replace that negative habit of being mean to yourself with a gentler approach, and practice sustaining it each moment.

I am greeting my refection with a softened gaze.

Usually we greet our refection in the mirror with a hard and critical eye. Our eyes scan the mirror each morning asking, "What's wrong with me today?" A new line, spot, gray hair? Next time, try softening your gaze. Allow love and kindness to infuse your gaze. You may be surprised by the love and beauty that wants to shine back at you.

I am giving myself permission to make beautiful mistakes.

People love this one!

While attending a Zen meditation retreat many years ago, I spoke with the meditation teacher, Joan Sutherland, Roshi, about my fear of moving forward in my writing and teaching. She asked me what was stopping me. I answered, "I am afraid of making a mistake." She asked me to consider that everything we do might be a mistake of sorts, and that it is our duty to make "the most beautiful mistake" we can in any situation, bringing the very best of ourselves to every decision.

If you are willing to make the most beautiful mistake that you can, given all the knowledge you have at that moment, then it will lead you to make the next most beautiful mistake, and so on. This advice freed me up enormously. Making "beautiful mistakes" over and over can liberate us from the obsession of being perfect and allow us to take the risks necessary to live life to the fullest.

You can also simplify this to, **"I am willing to have a go."** Nothing to lose, just do it for the fun of it!

I am my own compassionate witness.

Often it's not so hard to have compassion for the person beside you, or for the person halfway across the world. But how about compassion for yourself: not so easy sometimes, mostly because our first reaction when things go "wrong" is to chastise ourselves.

Next time, the moment before you resort to knee-jerk, not-so-kind behavior toward yourself, try taking a breath (full of warmth and kindness), step back from the situation, and see if you can be your own most compassionate witness . . . just for today.

I encourage you to have a relationship with these principles and to make them your own. Carry them around with you, calling them to mind often. Some may speak to you more than others. Give them a try and see what happens. Remember, you are worth it.

Playtime!

Use this play space to make up your own "Just for Today Principles":

- *Just for today* ______________________________
  ____
- *Just for today* ______________________________
  ____
- *Just for today* ______________________________
  ____
- *Just for today* ______________________________
  ____
- *Just for today* ______________________________
  ____

Beginner's Mind

If the angel deigns to come, it will be because you have convinced her, not by tears but by your humble resolve to be always beginning: to be a beginner.

~ Rainer Maria Rilke

You are invited to embark on this creative discovery with childlike curiosity and wonder. Be willing for the adult in you *not* to know so much. Let's begin this adventure with what Zen practitioners often refer to as "beginner's mind."

When we are beginners, there is room for delightful surprises and new information to emerge. When we think we have to know how things are "supposed" to go, we often want to stick to what we already know in order not to appear foolish to people around us. In my experience, this predictable behavior only serves the purpose of keeping us the same. There is no room for learning and expansion when we are overly concerned with how we look on the outside.

To help acquaint you with the power of the beginner's mind, we will explore four of its aspects:

1. Change and discovery;
2. Reaction or response;
3. The magic of edges; and
4. Asking for help.

Aspect 1. Change and Discovery

As we get started, I invite you to take a moment and recall all the changes (big and small) that you have already been through in your life.

We often forget to pause and honor where we are right now. No matter what opinion you have about yourself, you *have already* come a long way, baby!

Map It

Changes in My Life

You may want to record a few of these changes on the roadmap to remind yourself of how far you have already come. Consider family issues and other relationships, projects and work challenges, your health, and connection to the earth.

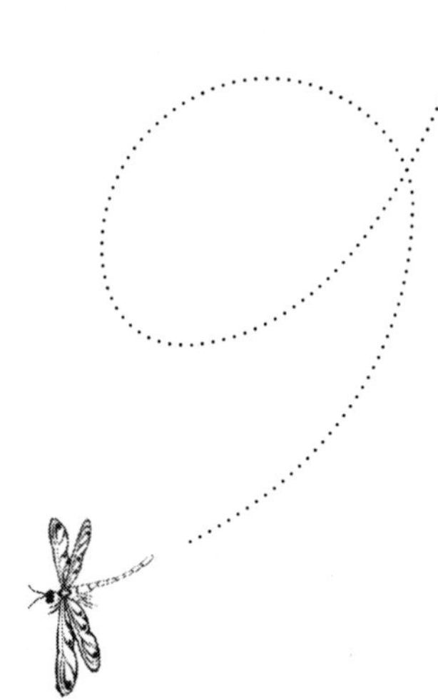

- *I used to fight with* ______________________ *(fill in the blank) constantly; now* ______________ ______________________________.

- *I used to* ______________________________;
  now ______________________________.

- *I used to* ______________________________;
  now ______________________________.

- *I used to* ______________________________;
  now ______________________________.

As we begin anything new, change is something that happens whether we like it or not. Many of us say we want it (you probably do, or you wouldn't be reading this right now), but at the same time we want to feel, with some degree of certainty, that we are going to be secure and comfortable. If you can accept that you are *not* going to feel comfortable all of the time, you can let go of a lot of unnecessary suffering during the process of change. Suffering is largely a result of *resisting* change and going against the flow.

Treasure the Moments

What I Like about Myself Today

Having taken a look back at the path you've traveled, take stock of where you are today. Name three things that are "right" about you, here and now. By *right* I mean acknowledging what you already like about yourself at this point in time. I encourage you to continue adding to this list throughout all the practices in this book.

- ______________________________

  is right about me, right now.
- ______________________________

  is right about me, right now.
- ______________________________

  is right about me, right now.

Change and discovery go hand in hand. Discovery usually requires us to be willing to move out of our comfort zones and risk feeling foolish for a while. Even our idols have done this—Albert Einstein said, "I never came upon any of my discoveries through the process of rational thinking."

You are cordially invited to step out of your comfort zone.

Please leave behind, or at least turn down the volume of, your inner critic and judge.

Please RSVP with your sense of humor and your curious mind.

Practice

Getting Personal and Honest

- What does your comfort zone look like?
- Is it totally satisfying?
- What is calling you out of your comfort zone?
- What possibilities do you imagine lie in your discovery zone?

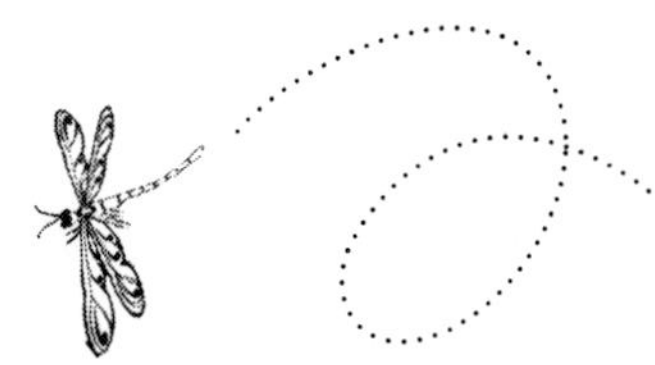

Use this starter example to begin your list. Revise it as you explore and discover new aspects of your creativity.

Comfort Zone	Discovery Zone
Cup o' joe in the morning while I read my emails	Walking out the door, first thing, to experience the light, the breeze, the smells
Saying, "I'm fine with that."	Saying, "I don't feel good about that and would like to talk about it."

Aspect 2. Reaction or Response

We often *react* from the past, triggered by memory, hurt, fear, betrayal, etc. There is no *new* life force in reacting from the past. Consider your own reactions by completing these statements:

- *When someone raises their voice, I feel* __________
  ____
  ____.

- *When asked my opinion, my immediate reaction is* _
  ____
  ____
  ____.

- *Sometimes I hesitate, wondering what will my mother, the neighbors, my boss, girlfriends* __________ *(fill in the blank) think if I* __________
  ____
  ____.

Past experiences can either serve to inform the decision-making process or hinder it. When we unconsciously react we are not pausing to check out the current set of circumstances. We are assuming that everything is exactly the same as before, which is seldom true.

When we consciously *respond* from the present moment, it is an act of creation. Your power is in the *now.*

Practice

Stopping to C

To see what is actually happening in the moment, to realize how you can create a response, take the "c" out of being reactive and put it first and foremost to be creative.

REACTIVE
CREATIVE

Come to the edge, he said. They said: We are afraid. Come to the edge, he said. They came. He pushed them and they flew.

~ GUILLAUME APOLLINAIRE

Positive change happens when you respond to the call of the moment from *here and now,* where your power is, instead of reacting from the past. It doesn't mean it's going to be a breeze to respond, but it does mean you are participating and co-creating with the moment. Now, that is cool! (And very often uncomfortable.) Here is another example:

> Ted sees the greasy frying pan still in the sink from last night and feels anxiety and anger at his wife. He takes a deep breath, steps back, and realizes: this pan has nothing to do with my mother getting drunk at night and neglecting me. This pan reflects the lovely, late dinner we shared last night, and neither of us felt like cleaning up. I can wash this pan in two minutes, and she'll be happy to see that I'm taking care of things.

Aspect 3. The Magic of Edges

Edges are juicy, interesting, and compelling. Edges hold possibility and high vibrations. Nature shows us this all the time. In permaculture, the edges between different vegetation contain the most life force.

Edges are mystical. Edges can also be scary.

Before you let fear keep you from the edge, consider that discoveries happen at the edges. Explore them!

Map It

Measuring the Edge

Take a few minutes to write down whatever occurs to you, not censoring any thoughts or images that may arise. Remember, you don't have to know all the answers right now. You may not know, and that is okay. You can always come back to this later. For now, notice whatever thoughts and feelings come up for you. Don't judge them. Just notice.

- *What feels edgy to you?* ______________________________

  ____

- *Where in your life are you playing it safe?* __________

  ____

- *What are you on the edge of right now?* ___________

  ____

- *Once you identify the edges in your life, notice what comes up for you. How do you feel?* _____________

  ____

Cultivating patience is vital for this process. Impatience readily rushes in and tells us we need to plan every step, so we can feel comfortable again. Impatience is not a friend of change. Patience—with yourself, with the nature of change—helps build trust that the next step will rise up to meet us.

Change is a natural part of any life cycle. Nature shows us that the darkest hour is before the dawn. Each new day rises from the dark of the night. Nature is constantly showing us that changes are taking place underground, invisible to the eye, long before we get to appreciate their manifestation.

Spring is here and
nobody knows how
it happened.

~ ANTONIO MACHADO

It is important to remember that changes can be taking place deep down inside of you, whether you can see them or not. Your willingness and ability to be at the edge will bring awareness of changes.

Because our senses are usually heightened at edges, we are more likely to notice signs and opportunities when they present themselves. When the time is right and the opening appears—*jump! Go for it!*

Forget safety.
Live where you
fear to live.
Destroy your reputation.
Be notorious.

~ RUMI

The comfort zone is overrated—move beyond it. Inch out, expecting to get a little nervous. Take a deep breath and discover that you feel proud of yourself for standing outside of your comfort zone. Instead of backing away from new encounters that could expand your sense of who you are, and why you are here, discover that you are bigger and stronger than you imagined.

Practice

Breathing!

Your breath can help you. Your breath can lead you there. Try this simple and effective exercise:

- Inhale slowly all the way to your belly, silently affirming, "I am breathing."
- Exhale slowly from your belly, silently affirming, "I am centered."
- Repeat this at least ten times or for as long as it takes to feel centered in yourself, wherever you are.

Begin to equate your comfort zone with your breath. Your breath is always accessible, and that means your center is always accessible, too.

Aspect 4. Asking for help

What if you could call out to an invisible and loving force, bigger than you, to accompany you on this journey into the unknown? It could be your guardian angel, an ancestor, a power animal, a friend (real or imagined), or your Higher Power, whatever that means to you. Some of you may already have a guide or support you call upon. Trusting your beginner's mind, giving yourself permission "not to know," you can call out for help with the understanding that there is nothing to prove.

Practice

Asking

I encourage you to take a few moments now and engage in a simple practice of summoning help: Imagine you are walking up a mountain that is made of pure and clear crystal. Once you get to the top you see a beautiful house that has a purple door, with golden rays of light pouring out from underneath the doorway. You pause for a moment, taking in a breath full of warmth and kindness, and silently ask your guides to open the door, when they are ready. Once the door opens, take a few moments to notice all the details. Ask your guides if they have names, and thank them for offering their assistance and love to you now and whenever you choose. Please know your guides are more than happy to assist you and are delighted to be asked for your help.

To ask for help requires a level of maturity, surrender, and humility, which your ego (small self) will protest against. Your ego wants you to think you should already know and will try to shame you into thinking that asking for help is a sign of weakness. Your ego wants you to stay where you are. It is afraid of change and doesn't like beginnings. Help can come when we have the courage to call out for it and the wisdom and humility to accept it when it comes, even when it comes in a way we were not expecting.

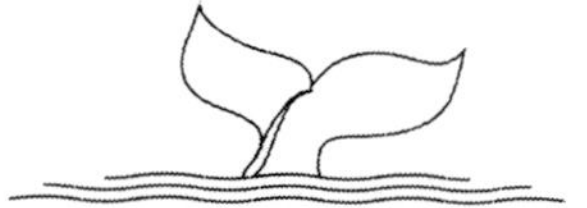

Treasure the Moments

Complete this phrase: I would like help with . . .
Example: I would like help with expressing myself.

- *I would like help with* ______________________________
____
____.

- *I would like help with* ______________________________
____
____.

- *I would like help with* ______________________________
____
____.

Congratulations, you have started!

2

The Practice of Not Knowing

Honoring the Unknown

> *It is by going down into the abyss that we recover the treasures of life. Where you stumble, there lies your treasure.*
>
> ~ JOSEPH CAMPBELL

If you knew there was no way you could possibly fail—what might you attempt?

Do you know what stops you from jumping in, going for it, living your bliss, and shining out into the world like you were born to?

Fear is what stops many of us. The fear of being uncomfortable, getting it wrong, or venturing into the darkness of the unknown. So we turn away from our hopes and dreams and settle into our comfort zones, even though we know there is more to life.

Usually where there is great fear, there is great potential. The more we keep these two aspects separate and apart, the more stress we create for ourselves. The more we wear blinders to potential, the more cut-off we become. Our comfort zone becomes a fortress that walls us off from the world, from others, from ourselves.

Practice

My Funky Fear List

What fears are keeping you stuck in your comfort zone? What potential is denied by these fears?

My fear of being wrong . . .	keeps me from speaking in public.
My fear of being seen . . .	keeps me from expressing my deepest thoughts and feelings.
My fear of being hurt . . .	keeps me from trusting others and experiencing intimacy.
My fear of	*Keeps me from*
My fear of	*Keeps me from*
My fear of	*Keeps me from*

Let's Get Acquainted

Now that all your worry and fear has proved such an unlucrative business, why not find a better job?

~ Hafiz

We all know what it feels like to be afraid and uncomfortable, and we don't particularly like it. Our tendency is to push the uncomfortable thing away. We often push our fears away and try to pretend they don't exist. We secretly hope that if we push them far enough away, they won't have control over us anymore. Very often these pushed-away fears can have far more control over us than we realize.

You will never be able to outrun your fears, and in my experience they do not just go away. They hang out, waiting to pounce, and usually surface just when you are on the edge of an exciting new possibility. They will always catch up with you. For that reason, I suggest doing something that may sound unpleasant at first: **invite them in.** Get to know them, one by one. Be willing to suspend the stories that validate and feed them. Ask questions of them. Get to know them. The more you know your fears, the less likely they are to have the power to control you.

So, how do we address not knowing? We ask questions!

I suggest you ask questions with the tone of a compassionate witness, full of warmth and genuine curiosity, as if you were trying to solve a mystery. (This might be a good time to review "Just for Today," from the first chapter.)

Don't stress out if you don't know the answers instantly. You probably won't. This practice is about exploring, not about knowing. As is the case with all of the practices in this book, you can come back to it later.

Practice

Questioning Your Fears

This is not a test. It is an opportunity to stay curious about what gets in your way and to understand that *you* are not your *fear*. Try the following questions to get started. Imagine you are speaking directly to your fear.

- What triggers you, calls you forth?
- Where did you come from?
- Whose voice do you show up with?
- Are you my fear or someone else's?
- What purpose have you served in the past?
- What purpose are you serving now?
- What would my life look like without you?

Sometimes when you are in a dark place, you think you have been buried, but actually you have been planted.

~ CHRISTINE CAINE

Escape Artist vs. Healing Artist

Instead of investing time in becoming the healing artist of our lives, we put a lot of energy into becoming an escape artist. We will go to great lengths to avoid looking at the very things that can set us free. But where, exactly, does this take us?

Unconsciously, over a lifetime, all of us have developed different strategies for living, and a lot of these strategies revolve around keeping our fears at bay. Some of these strategies include creating a very busy life for ourselves, a life full of distractions—such as constantly engaging with our cell phones, computers, social media, shopping, drinking, saving people—anything that will keep us from going deeper and help us to avoid looking at our fears.

Telling the fears to go away is another strategy. I have tried this one many times. It hasn't worked for me so far! They usually pop up again, just when I am on the verge of an exciting new possibility.

So even though we push our fears away and strategize to avoid looking at them, it doesn't mean they go way. We may think we are outrunning and escaping our fears, but they accompany us wherever we go. Very often, they get lodged deep in our hearts. They run the show from the dark corners of our psyche. They resurface in a place Buddhists call *ghost world*.

Ghost world is that place where all the *if onlys, I should/shouldn't haves,* and *not enoughs* reside and gather their energy. Ghost world operates at the edges of new opportunities, in the shadows and the dark places where we have consciously or unconsciously pushed away many or all of our fears and unwanted feelings. Ghost world keeps us running in the dark, taking us nowhere, keeping us stuck in the past, stuck in the land of shadows and regrets. It also keeps us running on empty, creating more distance from where we truly long to be.

If you don't break your ropes while you are alive, do you think ghosts will do it after?

~ Kabir

Most of the time we are unconscious of the existence of ghost world, unconscious of how we continuously feed it and keep it alive by pushing our fears and our discomfort away from us. Our busy lives keep us running away from the darkness, from our shadows, and ultimately away from our own hearts.

Many of us don't realize that by pushing our fears away, we are also pushing away our greatest discoveries.

Fear isn't the root problem. It is natural to feel fear. When a dog menaces, fear helps you avoid harm. When a storm rages, fear leads you to seek shelter. It is only when you label the fear *wrong* or *bad* that you want to push it away. The fear itself is not a problem. The problem arises when we take our fears for granted, reacting to them from the past, and getting stuck in the habits we have developed over years of trying to escape from them. "It is wrong to be afraid of speaking in public," we tell ourselves—and we push the fear out of consciousness while simultaneously side-stepping all opportunities to speak in public.

May your heart never be haunted by the ghost structures of old damage.

~ JOHN O'DONOHUE

What happens for you when fearful feelings start to rise? Take a minute and be honest with yourself. Do you shut down, go online, become irritable, depressed, work, drink, smoke, shop, or eat more? Start by identifying and noticing how you react. (No shame here whatsoever, folks—this is to help **you become bigger than the fear!**)

Take note of your answers as they arise, so you can identify what behaviors *feed your fears.*

Practice

Identifying My Negative Stories

Can you identify some of the beliefs you have banished to your own ghost world? Try this:

- *No one will like me if* ______________________________
____
____
______________________________.

- *I am not* ______________________________ *enough.*

- *Because I am not* ______________________________
______________________________ *, I can't or shouldn't*
____
______________________________.

- *I shouldn't be too* ______________________________ *because*
____
______________________________.

- *I am afraid to do what I love because*______________
____
____
______________________________.

Do you really believe that your fears and negative stories are totally and utterly true? Perhaps some of them were true or felt true in the past, but do they remain true today?

If there is even one percent of you that doesn't believe the negative story you have been telling yourself, that is enough. It provides a place to enter. When you are willing to question your stories and beliefs, you are on your way to healing them. You are also on your way to discovering that you are much bigger than your fears. You are on your way to becoming a healing artist.

Let's Get Intimate

As a budding healing artist, take a minute to read over the negative stories you identified above. Do they have anything in common? Is it possible these stories all originated in childhood? For most of us, childhood is ground zero for our fears and self-criticisms.

Where you ever afraid of the dark when you were a kid? Thought the boogey man was hiding under you bed? Sometimes all we needed was someone we trusted to come in and turn on the light. Once the light was on, we looked around and discovered that there was nothing or no one to be afraid of.

Unfortunately, for many, the fears and negative talk stay locked in the past. We each hold prisoner that inner child who never ages. We inhabit our adult selves and our past child selves, and remain reluctant to turn on the light. We have become accustomed to living in the dark, with our fears, and we get nervous about what might be exposed if we turn on the light.

Yet as adults we hold a great power. We can turn the light on for the inner child who never grew up. We can hold the hand of our inner child and shine the light not only on our fears but also on the beauty of our childhood selves.

Marianne Williamson illustrates this beautifully in her book, *A Return to Love*:

> *Our deepest fear is not that we are inadequate. Our deepest fear is that we are powerful beyond measure. It is our light, not our darkness, that most frightens us.*

Very often it can be our own magnificence and the thought of having an intimate relationship with life itself that scares us the most. It implies that we will have to stop playing small and show up as our truest self.

Having the courage to turn on the light invites us to have an up close and personal relationship with all of life, including our fears.

You can practice bringing your fears out of the darkness, befriending them, and treating them with kindness.

Contrary to what you might think, getting intimate is all about *not knowing*. Remember when you fell in love: the intimacy you nurtured was all about exploring that special, other person—and allowing them to explore you. For most of us, this is pretty uncomfortable at the start. But it's also exciting. Standing naked, face to face with the unknown—now that is intimate! But it also exposes us. Getting deeply intimate with our truth implies a kind of vulnerability, and that scares most of us.

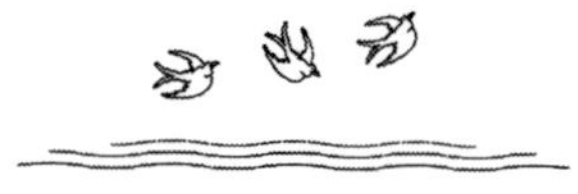

Playtime!

Boo!

For one week, do one thing every day that is out of your comfort zone. It could be anything from going out to eat by yourself, checking out a new class, rolling out a yoga mat, striking up a conversation with a stranger, running an extra mile, trying a new recipe, or skydiving. If you miss a day, no big deal, just come back to it.

Do one thing every day that scares you.

~ Eleanor Roosevelt

Get creative and give yourself permission to have fun with this. Jot down your observations about the experience.

Out of Comfort Zone Activity	Discovery Zone Observations
Monday	
Tuesday	
Wednesday	
Thursday	
Friday	
Saturday	
Sunday	

Well of Dreams

Have you ever gone to the edge of a well and looked in? It's deep and dark down there. What does someone usually do at a well? They take a coin out of their pocket, hold it tight, make a wish, throw it in, and walk away. Right?

We leave our dreams and wishes at the bottom of the well, forgotten in the darkness, and get on with our lives.

What if, at the bottom of all that darkness, there was something priceless just waiting for you to go deep down and discover?

All color, water, and life come from the darkness. What new discoveries want to be born from the darkness of your psyche?

Now is the time to remember your life's dreams and wishes. Dreams you once held close and then, either consciously or unconsciously, threw away.

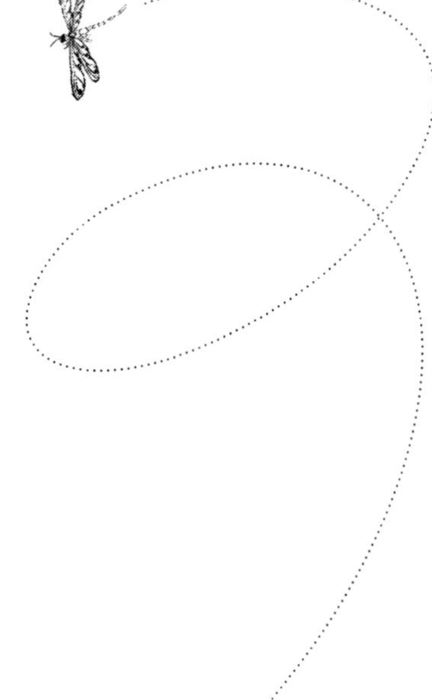

Playtime!

Waking Dreams

What do you dream and wish for today? Try this: go to your piggy bank or coin jar and extract a penny, a nickel, a dime, and a quarter. Use these coins to symbolize the wishes, hopes, ambitions, and dreams you want to bring to the surface of your life. Reality won't necessarily happen the way you wanted it to unfold, but by bringing your desires to the surface you can enter into a relationship with them and introduce them into your life in a new way. Getting intimate with your deepest longings will help you discover your deepest purpose, so you can start living it.

- *Penny – My wish for today is* ________________ ______________________________________ ______________________________________.
- *Nickel – My hope for tomorrow is* ____________ ______________________________________ ______________________________________.
- *Dime – My ambition for this year is* ___________ ______________________________________ ______________________________________.
- *Quarter – My dream for my life is* ____________ ______________________________________ ______________________________________.

Once you identify them, be careful not to discard them again by letting your rational mind tell you they will never manifest. That is up to you! You get to decide how you want to interact with them. For example, if you dream of becoming a famous singer but feel you missed the boat—just sing! Sing anywhere. Join a local choir or start your own. Volunteer at a nursing home or hospital to sing to patients. Sing for yourself. The important thing is that you keep the dream alive by bringing that activity into your life, no matter how it looks. Focus on how it makes you *feel* instead.

Welcoming Myths into Our Lives

Follow your bliss.

~ JOSEPH CAMPBELL

Myths are stories (kids love stories!) that are derived from ancient wisdom throughout the ages. They provide us with a larger framework than our own small stories, and a larger consciousness of the meaning of life itself. They make us remember that we are not alone. They can teach and guide us. For women, many tales of queens, heroines, goddesses, mothers, daughters, and wives illuminate trials we may have undergone in our own lives.

These magical stories are transformational journeys, which usually involve a descent to the underworld, banishment to a forest, or wandering in a desert. This period of exile, searching, and perseverance in unknown territory is always followed by an ascent and a returning, leaving the traveler changed and altered forever. Not so different from our own lives, is it? We can call upon the attributes and characteristics of mythological figures to accompany us and aid us in our own transformative journeys.

One of the many myths I like to work with is the myth of Psyche. This is a long and detailed adventure of a young woman's journey to the underworld and back. I encourage you to look up the full epic tale if it interests you. For now, I will briefly share the part of the story that relates to our next creative exercise.

> Psyche, a young and very beautiful mortal woman, has angered the Goddess Venus, known as the most beautiful woman in the universe. Venus sets out tasks for Psyche to perform, before she will reunite her with her beloved (who happens to be Venus's son, Eros, better known to us as

> Cupid—part of the reason why Venus is furious). One task requires Psyche to journey to the Underworld to retrieve a box of beauty that Venus needs in order to be complete. Even Venus, the most beautiful Goddess in the world, needs the beauty from the darkness to be whole.
>
> Along the journey Psyche is harassed by Venus's servants, who are aptly named Old Habit, Anxiety, and Grief. Psyche also gets some advice from a compassionate witness along the way who advises her that she will be offered the throne when she arrives, but not to take it. She does not need to become the Queen of the Underworld, she only needs to stay as long as it takes to retrieve the box of beauty, and not a moment longer. Once she has the box in her hands, she must return to the light immediately.
>
> *In the end, it works out well for Psyche. She falls asleep upon her return, exhausted from her adventure, and is eventually woken up by Eros (Love).*

No doubt you are already on your own epic journey and have ventured into unknown and dark territory, too. The myth of Psyche assures us that our searching and descent are not in vain. Beauty can be found and retrieved from the darkest and most unlikely places. We have to be willing to find it and return to the world, slightly altered and changed, then use it to help bring us into a more beautiful and loving relationship with ourselves, first, and then with everyone else.

Practice

Creating Your Beauty Box (or Treasure Chest)

Set aside at least an hour for this one. You will need a plain box, any shape or size you like. A shoebox works well, or you can buy a wooden or cardboard box at a craft store. Use your imagination and creative impulses to decorate it any way you like. Some people like to paint, others cover it with scrapbook paper, images from magazines, photographs, cut up cards they have received over the years—you name it!

Pay special attention to the inside, the part that is not so visible. Here are some questions to consider while making your beauty box. I encourage you to dig deep into your psyche and be willing to discover interesting and beautiful things about yourself and your life.

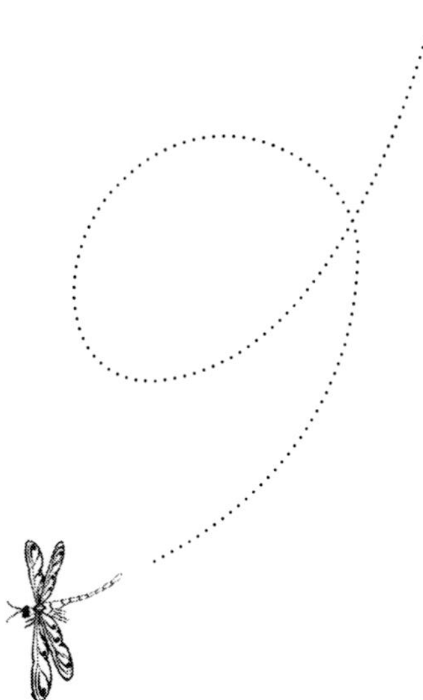

- What is beautiful to you?
- What do you want to bring to life?
- What seeds are you planting in the dark?
- What do you want to cultivate and grow in your life?
- What or whom inspires you?

There is no wrong way to do this, shake it up to suit you. Oh, yes, remember please: there is no particular way it is "supposed" to look. No two boxes have ever looked the same. Make it for *you,* to remind yourself that there is beauty in breakdown. You are living proof.

Elizabeth's Story

When I started on my Creative Discovery journey, I was working through early childhood trauma and the most recent trauma of the amputation of my fingers, due to a car accident. At first, I would sometimes get frustrated because I thought my artwork was not as "good" as the others in the group. To me it looked juvenile. However, as the weeks went by, that thinking subsided and I relaxed more into the creative process. I think I just got tired of telling myself I wasn't creative enough, since I was having fun just creating!

For me the most influential project was the beauty box. When I finished, I walked away happy with my work for the first time. I painted the box with colors that made me smile and decorated it with little mirrors, feathers, and shells. I lined the inside with red felt, purple glitter, and chocolate gold coins, to represent my dreams. Later I wrote positive words on rocks, and put them in the box, too.

Now I pull them out when my negative thinking starts to kick in, and they help me to remember that I am a lot stronger than I think I am. Finally, I traced my hand—without the fingers on it—and put it into the box, to remind myself how it does not make me ugly.

Practice

99 Reasons

Cut out ninety-nine slips of paper and choose a theme for your list. For example:

- ★ 99 reasons to follow your bliss
- ★ 99 reasons to dream
- ★ 99 reasons for living
- ★ 99 reasons for anything you like!

One by one, over time, label the empty slips and put them into your box. Once you have completed all 99, randomly pick one out every day and read it out loud, as inspiration for your day. Here are some examples:

- ❁ Because I can feel sand through my toes
- ❁ Because I love the sound of my own laugh
- ❁ Because cut grass smells so good
- ❁ Because I have a sister
- ❁ Because someone calls me mommy
- ❁ Because I want to learn Spanish
- ❁ Because I like the sound of the cello
- ❁ Because I like to sing

I beg you to be patient toward all that is unsolved in your heart and to try to love the ***questions themselves*** *like locked rooms and like books that are written in a very foreign language. Do not seek the answers, which cannot be given to you now because you would not be able to live them. And the point is, to live everything.* ***Live*** *the questions now.*

~ Rainer Maria Rilke

Living the Questions

In this chapter, we have practiced Not Knowing by honoring it, identifying our fears, exploring how to heal, and getting intimate with parts of ourselves we've pushed into the darkness—all to discover the strength and beauty of ourselves.

We conclude this practice with advice from Rilke, who invites us to be patient and curious with the questions in our hearts. We can do the same with the fears that block what is longing to be revealed to us.

Practice

Getting Intimate with Fear – Guided Meditation

One way to turn on the light is to meditate, but meditation often elicits fear and anxiety in people. If you are one of them, don't worry, you are not alone! Maybe you have a hard time focusing on your own or have tried to meditate in the past to no avail? It's okay, no need to worry—this is a guided meditation where you will be accompanied by my voice along the way. In the "The Practice of Resting" chapter, we will take a closer look at demystifying meditation to help you develop your own practice if you choose to.

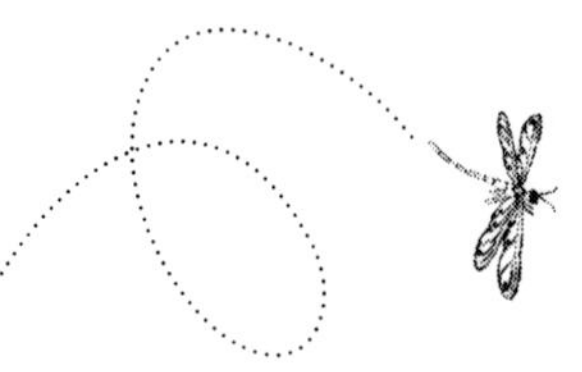

Free Guided Meditations

Please visit pashahogan.com/meditations to download your free guided meditations.

How to use this guided meditation:

- The Intimate with Fear meditation you download is something you can develop your own relationship with over time.
- I suggest you listen to this once in its entirety before you start practicing. **Practicing simply means noticing; noticing is the first step in interrupting habits.** This is a practice that keeps working with you as you change and grow.
- You get to decide how close and how long you want to stay with this meditation every time you do it.
- Listen to this often, picking it up and putting it down when you need to.

Entering into an intimate relationship with fear will ultimately bring you into a more intimate relationship with yourself and with all of the unknown possibilities this life has to offer.

**Remember,
every breath is a
new beginning!**

3

The Practice of Gratitude

> *Nothing is good or bad, but naming makes it so.*
>
> ~ William Shakespeare

Gratitude is an attitude. It is that simple. And it is a pretty great one. We have all heard the question, "Is your glass half empty or half full?" You get to decide. Sure, it is easy enough to be grateful when things are going your way. But what about the times when it doesn't feel so great? Not so easy, right? To be truly grateful is to move to a place beyond likes and dislikes, beyond *shoulds* and *shouldn'ts*, beyond right and wrong. Instead, dwell in the "What is."

We are usually quick to judge a situation or outcome as good or bad. It is good if it makes us feel good instantly and not so good if we don't like how it makes us feel. But how do we really know what is good or bad in the bigger picture? Similarly, we are grateful if things go the way we want them to or the way we think they are supposed to, according to our likes and dislikes, which are largely informed by cultural influences. This thinking only serves to limit our experience of ourselves and of the world at large.

Western culture is not set up to cultivate contentment. We are constantly bombarded with images and messages that suggest life will be better if we make more money, achieve more, accumulate more stuff, and keep striving for a new and improved version of ourselves according to the latest fad.

What if you could accept what is, practice contentment, and say thank you? I believe that is one of the highest, and most challenging, spiritual practices we can engage in.

There is a spiritual law: *The more you have and are grateful for, the more that will be given to you.*

Can you imagine what it would look like to practice gratitude for one full day? Have you ever tried? We are going to explore practicing "great attitude," one day at a time, every day.

Heads up: this will transform your life.

I'm speaking not just of material things but also of an abundance of joy, peace, happiness, and contentment with the present moment, no matter what is happening.

Imagine suspending your limited thinking for one day and simply accepting every situation as an unknown blessing and something to be grateful for. No matter what it is.

Are you willing to try it?

Practice

Treasuring the Moments

Let's keep it simple and take a moment to write down five things you are grateful for right now.

1. *I am grateful for* ____.

2. *I am grateful for* ____.

3. *I am grateful for* ______________________________
____.

4. *I am grateful for* ______________________________
____.

5. *I am grateful for* ______________________________
____.

The above can be the start of a list I invite you to add to every day until the page is full. Then you can start another one. It doesn't matter if you repeat what you are grateful for—that shows what truly matters to you.

I encourage you to do it at the same time every day for the next thirty days. You pick the time.

Your Promissory Note

For the next thirty days I, ________________, promise to take a few moments to pause, take a deep breath full of gratitude for the present moment, and on the exhale, write down one thing I am grateful for today. I will do this for five breaths.

Signed by: ____________________________

Date: _______________

Living Life According To vs. Living Life In Search Of

There is no meaning to life except the meaning man gives to his life by the unfolding of his powers.

~ ERIC FROMM

A major distraction from living in the moment is the narrative of our *shoulds* and *should'nts*. Every five seconds a new philosophy on life seems to beam out at us from social media sites, billboards, and commercials. They keep coming because, to quote my favorite Irish rock star Bono, "we still haven't found what we're looking for."

What are you looking for?

The brilliant American philosopher Richard Rorty (1931–2007) offered many perspectives on how we can view the world and live our lives. He wrote and lectured extensively on this subject and is widely known for his book, *Philosophy and the Mirror of Nature* (1979).

When you live your life "according to" there are many *shoulds* and *shouldn'ts*. Your life is reduced to a linear path, with lots of measuring sticks along the way to let you know how you are doing. For example: By the time you are twenty-one years old you should have figured out how you are going to make a living. By the time you are in your thirties you should have found a life partner and purchased your first home. By the time you reach forty-five you should have saved $X amount for your retirement.

Education, appearance, children, career, how much money you make, where you live, how you dress, where you shop—all the bases are covered. In this way of looking at life, it is important to have a plan. You know where you are supposed to be by a certain time in your life, and if you haven't reached it, the implication is that you are doing something wrong. It varies from culture to culture, but most of the time the programming is so deeply ingrained that we don't notice it. We take these benchmarks for granted and don't bother to question where they came from in the first place.

Sadly, the measuring gauge has already been determined by a force outside of you. It could range from and include any or all of these, and lots more: your family of origin, your friends, your village, media, advertisers (who want you to feel bad so you will buy their product or service), government, banks. The list is endless.

Living life "according to" implies that there is a certain way life is supposed to go, within a certain time frame, and by a certain set of criteria that measures our "success." Rarely do we meet these standards. There appears to be a gap between where we are and where we *should* be, leaving us feeling frustrated and annoyed with ourselves.

Practice

Deconstructing the Ruler

Are you aware of the ways "according to" has been operating in your life so far?

Identify your "According To" limitations here: (be as specific as you can)

For example:

- According to the fashion magazines, I should be ten pounds lighter.

- ❀ According to my parents, I should be further along in my career.
- ❀ According to my friends, I should own my house by now, be married, have children.

Room for yours!

- ❀ *According to* ______________________________
  I should __________________________________ .
- ❀ *According to* ______________________________
  I should __________________________________ .
- ❀ *According to* ______________________________
  I should __________________________________ .
- ❀ *According to* ______________________________
  I should __________________________________ .
- ❀ *According to* ______________________________
  I should __________________________________ .

Most of us are unconsciously living this way, feeling like we are not quite measuring up and are not enough. Sound familiar?

Even worse, when we do make the grade, complacency can settle in and limit our potential and our deepest aspirations.

Good news! There is another way to live. Lots of ways, actually, but check this one out for starters.

Living Life *In Search* Of

No straight road, no measuring device—this one looks more like a labyrinth. There is a way in, through, and out, but each person has a unique path. No one knows how long it takes to get anywhere; it doesn't really matter. What matters is that you understand that wherever you are in the journey is exactly where you are supposed to be, and wherever you are right now is your greatest possibility for growth and transformation. Right now—your greatest opportunity, no matter if it presents itself in a pleasing or unpleasant way to your ego. Make the present moment your best friend. Say "YES!" to now and to life, however it shows up.

Living life "in search of" entails learning from your experiences and bringing that wisdom forward into your life. There is no recipe to follow and no "according to" to stray from. The life you are living right now is not a detour until something better comes along. There are no detours! Nothing is a detour and absolutely *everything* is your greatest possibility in that search for a fulfilling and rich life—even, especially, the parts you want to rush past so you can get on with the rest of your life, with the life you think you are supposed to be living, according to others.

This path can feel dangerous and scary. It is! It takes great courage and a radical shift of perception. It will certainly rock the people-pleasing ground beneath your feet. Bolster your commitment to creative discovery by reviewing some of the earlier practices for Beginning and for Not Knowing. When you're ready, move forward into NOW. Whether you know or don't know the answers to the following questions, they will guide you along your path of discovery. You can trust that what you know (or don't) will be revealed and change along the way.

Practice

Treasuring Now

- *What are you in search of?*
- *What does success mean to you, personally?*
- *What would you do if there were no way you could possibly fail?*
- *What experience do you ache to have?*
- *What activities bring you joy?*
- *Who are your biggest cheerleaders?*
- *Who inspires you?*
- *Whom do you inspire?*
- *Whom would you like to inspire?*

Notice how your answers to these questions shed light on things you value in life. Once you can live in the *now,* you can more fully live life in gratitude. You get to notice and to choose: a life full of "according to" or a life full of gratitude?

This is a daily practice, and believe me: it takes practice! Adopting this attitude means that there are no detours, no good days, no bad days, no going backward. It means your life gets larger as you let go of self-created illusions that limit your experience of yourself in the world. It means that you start to live a life full of possibilities, saying, "Yes!" and "Thank You!" for each moment. It means that life is no longer happening to you. You are actively participating in whatever situation you find yourself in by saying *yes* and *thank you*.

Blessings and Prayer

How do you practice gratitude? As noted above, there is a spiritual aspect to gratitude. As Rumi has told us, *"There are hundreds of ways to kneel and kiss the ground."* Other people liken gratitude to prayer. How do you pray?

If the only prayer you ever say in your life is thank you, it will be enough.

~ Meister Eckhart

There is no right or wrong way to pray. Take a moment to reflect upon what the word *pray* means to you. The word is often associated with the humble resolve to give thanks. To praise. To praise life. You don't have to make it any more complicated than that.

You can consciously decide to make your life a prayer by praising each breath. Our breath is our connection to life. The first thing we do when we are born is take in a breath, and the last thing we do before we die is exhale and let go. Breathing consciously can be a praising of life and in turn a beautiful prayer—if we let it. We can welcome each breath as a gift from beyond, with humility and love. When we exhale it can be an opportunity to release whatever is troubling us, surrendering it up to something bigger than ourselves. Breathing with this attitude and not taking any breath for granted can help soften our hearts and calm our minds. A calm mind is a creative mind.

Practice

Treasuring Your Breath

When you focus on what you have, your ABUNDANCE increases. I started with my breath. Noticing being alive is a good start.

~ OPRAH WINFREY

Take a moment and place both hands over your heart. With both hands on your heart *Breathe in Love: Exhale Gratitude.* Gradually slow down your breathing and allow yourself to connect with the sensation of your breath entering and leaving your heart.

As you repeat this breathing, imagine and feel your heart softening. A softened heart is a grateful heart. A grateful heart has no limitations.

How Do You Bless?

The deepest longing of human nature is to be seen, validated, and understood. To truly see someone is to bless them. We can bless people by how we meet them. In the Indian culture, one ancient and popular greeting is "Namaste." It means: "The Light inside of me sees the Light inside of you" (or "The God in me sees the God in you"). It is a recognition that the person you are beholding is a sacred being, worthy of acknowledgement.

The greeting of an indigenous tribe in South Africa is "Sawa Bona," which means: "I see you." The response, "Sikhona," means, "I am here." Basically, it implies that I exist because you see me. To see, and in turn to acknowledge being seen, creates and completes the circle of communion in the meeting.

These cultures, along with most indigenous people, understand how important it is to have an exchange of recognition and reciprocity. Imagine if we greeted one another with that same reverence and praise, as opposed to, "Hi. How are you?" "I'm fine. How are you?" Both greeting and response are usually offered without either party waiting for a genuine response. Most of us don't want to know how the other is doing. Most of the time we are too preoccupied with where we are going, what time it is, and what we have to do before we get there. We don't expect or even care about a genuine response. As a result, we walk around self-absorbed in our own thoughts, without seeing the unique and magnificent being looking back at us.

We do the same with ourselves—all too often. How often do you look in the mirror with warmth and curiosity? Have you ever? Most of us look in the mirror each morning and several times a day, without seeing who is looking back. We greet our own reflection by scanning the mirror with a critical eye, identifying quickly the slightest imperfection. Noticing only what strays from the idea of what we think we are supposed to look like. We zone in and focus intensely with a hardened eye on the proclaimed imperfection, so quick to judge the whole picture as a disaster! Seldom do we greet our own reflection with a softened gaze, beholding the person looking back at us. Our hard ideas and critical eye cloud our view, making it difficult for a softer, less judgmental eye to enter.

We have become so accustomed to looking at ourselves in this way that we are not even conscious of how much it affects our lives. If we don't see ourselves with love, respect, and gratitude, how can we possibly recognize another?

Yes, I know you practiced this one in the first chapter, but it's worth repeating here: Go back to the first chapter and reaffirm: *Just for Today: I am greeting my reflection with a softened gaze.*

Practice

Being Grateful for You

Each morning when you wake up, you have an opportunity to see yourself in a new way. This practice starts with blessing yourself every morning. You can do this by simply saying, "Yes, thank you! Anything is possible today," and really believing it.

Do this for thirty days and see how it impacts your life.

Practice

Softening the Gaze Meditation

I suggest you practice this guided meditation by following this link: pashahogan.com/meditations. (If you downloaded the Intimate with Fear meditation in the previous chapter you already have it.) I am also including the meditation in written form below, as many people have found it useful.

Before you get started with this meditation, take a few moments to soften the scene. It is important to find a space that is comfortable to you, where you won't be disturbed for at least twenty minutes.

You will need a mirror, preferably full-length. You may even want to light some candles.

Take your time, getting into a comfortable seated position in front of the mirror.

Pause.

Begin by noticing any resistances that may arise in having the mirror in front of you.

It's normal for resistances to come up right now.

Just notice them without letting them stop you from continuing the meditation.

Keeping your eyes open, take a few deep breaths.

Pause.

Imagine that each inhalation is filling your body with warmth and kindness.

Each exhalation is creating more space for warmth and kindness to enter your body.

Breathing deeply, you begin to get into a warmer and kinder relationship with your whole body.

Looking into the mirror, notice any thoughts, any feelings that may be coming up.

Just notice them, and bring your attention back to the slow and steady rhythm of your breathing.

Keep your focus on the next warm and soft inhalation, the next warm and soft exhalation.

Allow your breath to lead the way instead of your thoughts.

Notice how your inhalation matches the softness of your exhalation.

Breathe softly and steadily.

Breathe yourself into a kinder relationship with the person in the mirror.

Stay with your breath.

Together we will count to five . . . and then close your eyes. Begin counting at the end of each exhalation.

Pause.

Now close your eyes, focusing on your breath as it enters and leaves your body. Breathe SOFTNESS IN AND ALL AROUND YOU.

Receive your breath and allow it to soften any tension in your face. Your warm breath slowly caresses away any tension in your face.

Feel your breath slowly moving into your shoulders.

Let your shoulders drop and relax, sinking into your softened breath.

Stay with your breath, feeling your breath gently moving into your chest, feeling the warmth of your breath filling your entire chest.

Slowly breathe softness into your heart, softening and expanding your heart to fully receive your breath.

Each exhalation gently floats out of your body, creating more space to receive the next breath, full of warmth and kindness toward yourself.

The softness of your breath dissolves any hardness, any defenses around your heart.

Soften the guards, creating room for moments of happiness to emerge.

Create more room to receive the loving energy of your breath that is always present and available to you.

Breathe fully and softly.

Feel this loving energy floating down your body.

Your breath leads the way, into your belly, softening your belly to receive the next warm breath.

Let go of any hardness, any resistances to softening in and around your belly.

Let go of any judgments, letting it all go effortlessly with your breath.

Relax fully into your softened body.

Become aware of how your breath is breathing you.

Become aware of how easily your breath runs down the front of your legs and back up your spine.

Everything is relaxing into your softened breath, your softened body, this softened space.

Enjoy feeling how this softness fully supports you.

With your eyes still closed, internalizing your gaze, looking inside, see how much space there is for tenderness to emerge.

See how much space there is for compassion to emerge.

See how much space there is for forgiveness to emerge.

See how much space there is for gratitude to emerge.

See how much space there is for everything to emerge into this softened space.

See how much space there is for your soul to emerge.

Listen with a softened ear.

Listen to the whispering of your soul.

You are enough. You are enough.

Right now, you are enough.

Listen.

Receive.

Believe.

Continue to absorb these feelings for the next few minutes.

Pause for as long as you like.

Softly open your eyes and greet the beautiful stranger in the mirror who has loved you your whole life.

Sink into your eyes and gaze softly, full of warmth and curiosity.

Be your own most compassionate witness as you gaze into your own eyes.

Gaze and breathe, accepting the entire image.

There is room for all of you to emerge into this softened space.

Allow Grace to emerge and accompany you, just for today.

Stay with your breathing.

Stay with the softening, gazing, accepting.

Merge with your reflection, with your soul.

Softness fills the space all around you.

As we close the meditation, raise your hands and gently place your left hand over your heart and place your right hand on top. Breathe into your heart and feel how much love there is for you in this moment as you gaze at your own reflection.

Allow a smile to spread across your face.

Pause.

Moving your hands together, palm to palm, gently bow your head to your heart.

Bow humbly to the great power of this softness and honor yourself for taking the time to do this meditation.

When you leave this space, carry this softness out into your life.

Greet whomever you meet with a softened gaze, a softened ear, a softened heart—for you don't know what harsh commentators may accompany them.

To bless yourself is to be willing to truly meet yourself and have compassion for whatever you see. It is about blessing your whole life, even the parts you are not so crazy about. Reject nothing; everything is your greatest possibility to receive and give blessings, transforming your relationship with yourself, others, and your environment.

Practice

Counting Your Blessings

Aim for ninety-nine! Put this list someplace you can see it every day. (You can also write them on strips of paper and add them to your beauty box from the Practice of Not Knowing.)

Being truly grateful for what you see right in front of you is one of the most humbling things you will ever experience. To live in a state of gratitude and wonder will bring you to your knees. Let it.

Start with nine for now:

1. *Breathing is a blessing.*
2. ______________________ *is a blessing.*
3. ______________________ *is a blessing.*
4. ______________________ *is a blessing.*
5. ______________________ *is a blessing.*
6. ______________________ *is a blessing.*
7. ______________________ *is a blessing.*
8. ______________________ *is a blessing.*
9. ______________________ *is a blessing.*

Playtime!

Create a Blessing Flag

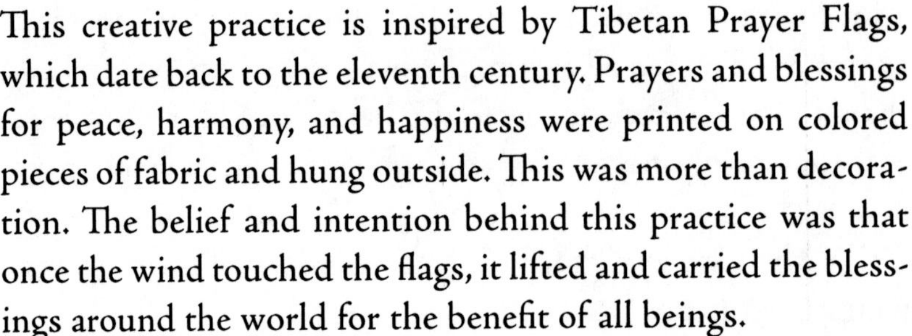

This creative practice is inspired by Tibetan Prayer Flags, which date back to the eleventh century. Prayers and blessings for peace, harmony, and happiness were printed on colored pieces of fabric and hung outside. This was more than decoration. The belief and intention behind this practice was that once the wind touched the flags, it lifted and carried the blessings around the world for the benefit of all beings.

You can make your own set of Blessing Flags to hang inside or outside your own home, to remind you how powerful it is to bless and to be blessed.

The Celtic tradition tells us that if we send a blessing out from our heart, it is multiplied and returns to bless us in return.

You will need:

- ★ Several pieces of white and colored fabric, which you will use for the flags.
- ★ Fabric markers.
- ★ Needle and thread and/or fabric glue.
- ★ A cord to attach the flags to.

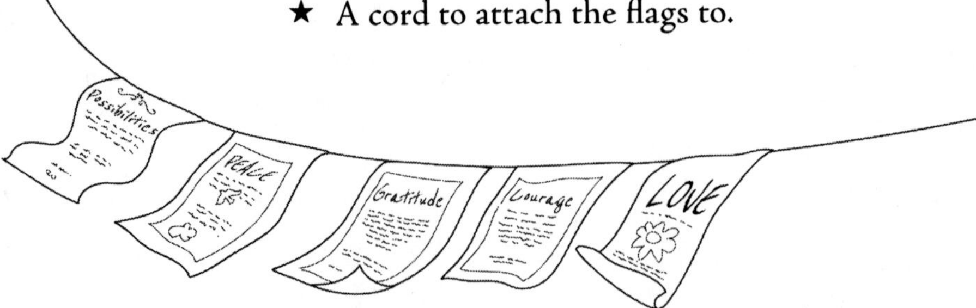

Suggestions on making your flags:

1. Cut the colored pieces of cloth slightly bigger than the white ones so they are big enough to frame the white cloth. You can decide how big you want the pieces to be, depending on where you want to hang them. I suggest making at least eight flags to string together. You can make as many as you like!
2. On the white pieces of cloth, with your fabric markers, you can write and/or draw messages of hope and encouragement to yourself or anyone you choose, with the intention of sending them out to the world. Refer back to your list of blessings for inspiration.
3. The white pieces of cloth can then be sewn or glued to the colored pieces of fabric. You only need to attach the top edge of the white piece to the colored piece of cloth. Make sure you leave an edge on the top of the colored pieces of cloth so you will be able to sew them onto the string later.
4. Take your string and lay out each flag, with a gap of a couple of inches between each. Make sure you have enough room on each side of the first and last flag so you can hang the flags from wherever you choose.
5. Now you can sew the top edge of each flag onto the string, making sure to go through the fabric and the string so they don't move around.
6. Stand back and look at your beautiful creation!
7. Hang the flags wherever you like. I suggest choosing a place where you will see them often. They can remind

you that you are connected to a much bigger world. A world that is grateful for your blessing.

Each day offers us the gift of being a special occasion if we simply learn that, as well as giving, it is blessed to receive grace and a grateful heart.

~ Sarah Ban Breathnach

The biggest blessing you can extend to the world is your resolve to show up each day with an attitude of gratitude. A soft and grateful heart and gaze leaves more room for possibilities and new discoveries to surface.

You may just discover that you have more to be thankful for and more to give to the world than you ever imagined.

Your willingness to see your true self is a blessing to all of us.

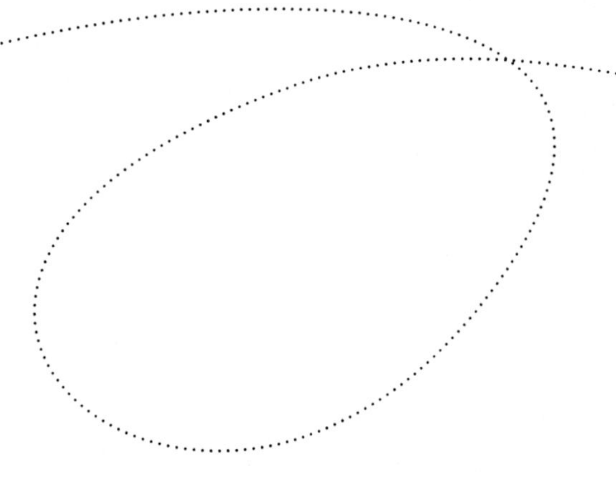

4

The Practice of Creating Sacred Space

> *Now is the time to remember that everything you do is sacred.*
>
> ~ Hafiz

The word *sacred* can mean different things, for a variety of reasons that can be attributed to our upbringing and religious beliefs. In the context of this practice, I invite you to put to rest any limiting beliefs you may be subconsciously applying to the word *sacred* and instead awaken the perception that sacredness is accessible to you in each moment. Anything or anyone can become sacred the instant we perceive their connection to Spirit, to something bigger than what is visible to the eye and understandable to the mind. The Irish poet, John O'Donohue, beautifully describes *sacred* as "where the holy invisible becomes visible."

The holy invisible, in our everyday and ordinary lives, has a better chance of becoming visible when we can unclutter our minds from our habitual way of seeing and thinking. We do that by creating sacred space both internally and externally in our everyday lives.

It is important to understand that sacred does not have to be some far-away thing, reserved only for very holy people. You are already sacred, right now. There is nothing you could have ever done in the past that can take *that*—your sacredness—away from you. This isn't a practice of *becoming* holy. It is a practice allowing you to *experience* who you already are.

Sacred space is a threshold. Discoveries love thresholds! They are born from them. A threshold is an opening where the known and the unknown merge. What seems impossible to the rational mind can become a possibility at a threshold. They are magical places, real and imaginary, where we can take time out from our racing thoughts and demanding lifestyles. Sound good? It gets better.

Once you are willing to lay down your burdens (*shoulds, not good enoughs, according tos,* all the harsh voices in your head), you can take refuge in your sacred space—ultimately, in yourself—as often as you like.

In order for this to work, you have to want it. If you don't want it, you won't practice attaining it. Give yourself permission to take the time to practice. You have to be willing to turn toward peace for sacred space to open.

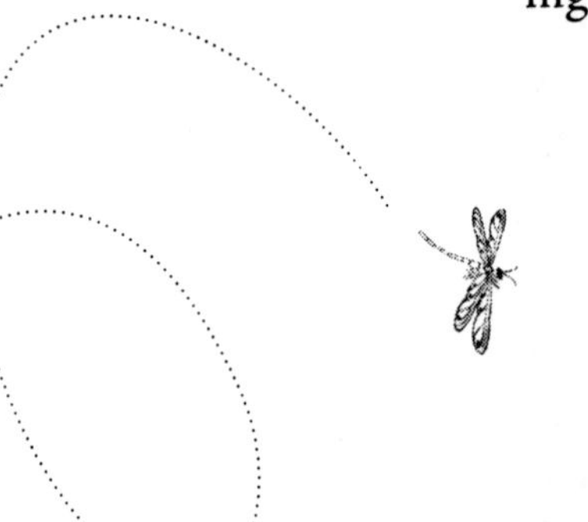

Playtime!

Granting Yourself Permission

Fill in your own **Permission Slip**. Print this out and post it where you can see it, to remind yourself that it is okay for you to tend to your soul. It can be especially useful when your impatient and conditioned mind kicks in and starts protesting. Be ready to recognize that critical voice when it pipes up, and don't give into it. It's not a matter of *if* or what excuse or condemnation your mind shouts out, it's a matter of *when* and *how* harsh.

Permission

I, ______________________________, give myself permission to spend at least ________ minutes each day in my Sacred Space. I am worthy of creating this space and taking this time for myself.

Signature: ___________________________
Date: ______________

This is a waste of time! I could be doing ____________
______________________________________ right now!

The list of what you "could be doing" is endless. The time you have designated to spend in your sacred space is not. Use it; you are worthy.

There is nothing wrong with you. It's not your fault. We are conditioned as human "doings." *Doing* is far more acceptable than *being* in Western culture.

There is a place for doing. In order to practice something you have to *do* it. I refer to that throughout this workbook. However, there is a difference between doing something that distracts you from your goal and doing something that brings you closer to the truth of who you are. It is up to you to learn how to discern the difference. It takes practice. Be kind and gentle with yourself in the process and you will know.

Most of us need to regularly spend time at a threshold before we move forward. It takes great courage to enter a threshold, to say to the universe that you are ready to turn down the critical voices in your head and attune your ear to listen for a new voice—one that is quiet and gentle and true to the call of your soul. This is the voice that will beckon you out of your comfort zone.

Once you cross, you are consciously leaving behind the known and entering into the unknown. Spending time in sacred space—internally and externally—helps to prepare our hearts and minds to be open to discovering what is on the other side.

Okay, here we go!

Internal Sacred Space

Let's start clearing space from the inside. It is often said that the body is a temple. That implies that the heart is the altar. What are you holding in the altar of your heart at this moment? Is it anger, resentment, worry, and fear? Or is it full of calm, forgiveness, joy, and gratitude? A mixture, maybe?

Take a few minutes to check in with your heart: place both hands over it, close your eyes, and breathe warmth and kindness into your chest. As you feel your chest expand, notice any feelings, emotions, sensations, or thoughts that arise. Gather anything that does not serve your highest self in this moment, then take both hands off of your chest and offer what doesn't belong to the wind, to the holy invisible, sending them away for this time so you can clear space in your heart for that which *does* serve you.

Of course, these things won't go away forever. However, by acknowledging how you are feeling in this moment and being willing to release distracting thoughts and feelings, for the time being, you can secure a few moments of peace. You can rest here for as long as you like and follow with this simple, effective breathing practice.

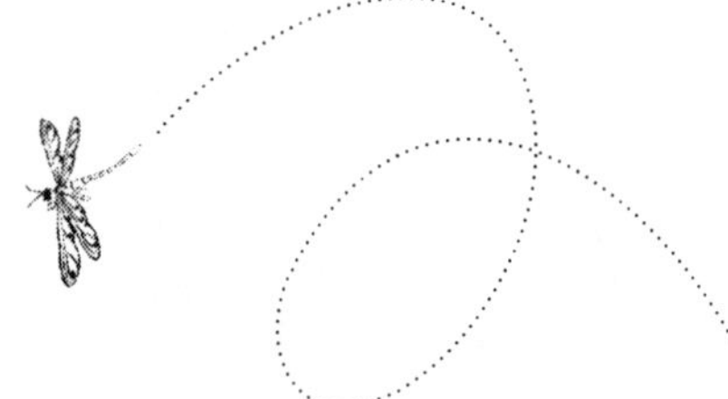

Practice

Stress-busting Breathing

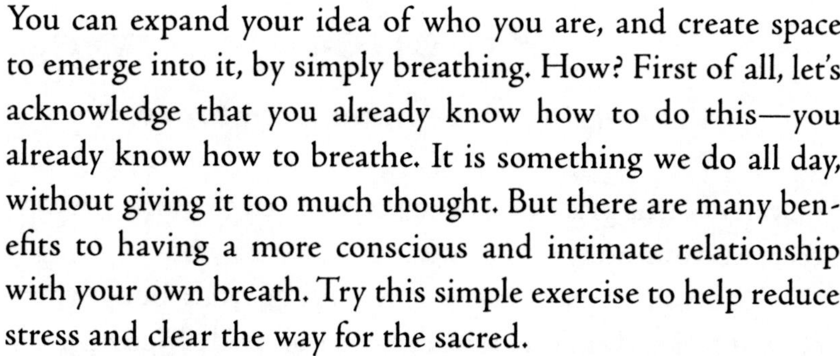

You can expand your idea of who you are, and create space to emerge into it, by simply breathing. How? First of all, let's acknowledge that you already know how to do this—you already know how to breathe. It is something we do all day, without giving it too much thought. But there are many benefits to having a more conscious and intimate relationship with your own breath. Try this simple exercise to help reduce stress and clear the way for the sacred.

Imagine on your next inhale that you are breathing in warmth and kindness. Warmth and kindness are flooding your entire body as you slowly and steadily inhale. Gently let go on the exhale. Placing one hand on your heart and the other on your belly, notice how your body gently rises on the inhale and falls on the exhale. As you continue breathing, you can begin to feel your heart and belly softening to receive the next breath.

Now let's add a breath count. Inhale to the count of four, exhale to the count of four. Inhale to four, exhale to five. Inhale to four, exhale to six. Inhale to four, exhale to seven. Inhale to four, exhale to eight. Continue inhaling to four, exhaling to eight for a few more breath cycles or as long as you like. Then, when you are ready, keep the inhale to four and exhale to seven, gradually counting your way back down, inhaling and exhaling to four.

By doubling the count of the exhale, you are sending a message to the parasympathetic nervous system to slow down. When we slow down our breath, we automatically slow down our stress-inducing thoughts.

Practice

Visualizing Your Inner Sanctuary

You can use this practice whenever you need to quickly reconnect with your body and to what is sacred to you.

With your mind's eye, find a place in your body where you want your inner sanctuary to be located. Many people choose the heart or belly, but it doesn't have to be there; it's your sanctuary.

Recall or imagine a place, in nature preferably, where you feel safe and surrounded by beauty. Perhaps it's a magical forest, beach setting, grassy meadow, or mountaintop. The little child inside of you also loves this place and is very happy to be here. In fact, it can be helpful to have your little one with you whenever you go here. Notice everything about this place. How does it smell, feel, look, sound? Are you alone or are there others present? What colors are most vibrant? Are you sitting, standing, or lying down? See yourself there in present time. Create this place in as much detail and color as possible. Take your time and breathe deeply into the part of your body where it is located. It is okay if you don't get a clear visual of it. What is most important is that you can create a warm and safe feeling inside of yourself.

Now that you have consciously created this place, you can go there at any time, especially when you need to ground, center, or feel safe in an instant.

Describe in writing, with as much detail as possible, what your internal sacred space looks like, feels like. Can you draw it? Collage it?

I suggest giving it a name or a sound that will help you remember that you can go there whenever you need to.

External Sacred Space

It is also important for you have access to a physical space that you can go to on a daily basis to rest, rejuvenate, and feed your creative heart and soul. For this reason, I suggest you find a place in your house that you can call your own. It doesn't have to be a huge space, just somewhere you can sit by yourself and rest. We will look at setting up a simple altar in this place in a moment. First, let's get the space ready.

The Importance of Ritual

The ancient practice of performing rituals has sadly been lost to many of us throughout the years. In today's quick-paced and rapidly changing world it is more important than ever to engage in practices that invite us to pause and consciously remember what is sacred to us, bringing positive intention into our actions.

Rituals can help us to clear and cleanse a space that you can claim and pronounce sacred. They also connect us to something bigger and give us a sense of belonging to a broader community.

A ritual is different from a habit because we do it consciously, with the intention of reaching out to touch what is sacred. You can make it an art form by getting creative with how you choose to do it. Here are some examples:

- You can light a candle, welcoming the Light into your space. Burn sage, incense, or essential oils such as rose, lavender, peppermint, frankincense, juniper, or cedar, to name a few.
- Break up old energy frequencies with a sound, such as clapping your hands, ringing a bell, or even humming or singing a song.
- Open a window, letting old energies out and a fresh breeze in.

We are often reluctant to engage in activities that could lead to more long-lasting happiness; how can this be? In our normal way of life we let ourselves be controlled by powerful thoughts and emotions, which in turn give rise to negative states of mind. We must deliberately take a stand and replace them with new habits and nurture new ways.

~ Dali Lama

Play with some of these or make up your own. It's more about pausing in your regular routine and setting the intention to create sacred space. Our positive thoughts are very powerful, even more so than negative ones. Energy follows thought. What you think about gets bigger, whether positive or negative! Think *threshold*.

Research shows that it takes at least thirty days to break a habit. Conversely, it takes the same amount of time to form a new one. Practicing your rituals for thirty consecutive days will help create new healthy habits. Here are examples of daily rituals that you can adapt, as needed, to the natural rhythm of your day.

Practice

Establishing a Morning Ritual

Each morning for the next thirty days, before you turn on your computer, phone, or anything else that beeps, go to your sacred place and sit there for at least five minutes. You can build this time up over the thirty days to twenty minutes. (Plan ahead and set your clock a little earlier.) Engage in your "Resting Meditation" practice and welcome in all the unknown blessings the day has to offer you. It's a brand new day—anything is possible. Anything! You just have to get your little self out of the way and be open to shaking up your routine.

Every breath can be an invitation to create sacred space in and around you. Every breath can be a prayer.

During this time, take a few moments to set a positive intention for yourself and your day. Let your intention come from your heart. An intention can give us direction and purpose, while at the same time can be flexible enough to flow with the river of the day.

Practice

Establishing a Daytime Ritual.

Intention also requires an action from us to bring it to life and infuse it with positive life-force energy. So write down your intention on a postcard. Use crayons, markers, colored pencils, or decorate the card with a design or symbol if you like. You can do this in two minutes and bingo: you're on your way to creating your own intention card deck!

Today I intend to . . . *smile often.*

. . . *practice random acts of kindness.*

. . . *remember to breathe.*

. . . *practice compassion with myself.*

. . . *love more!*

. . . *laugh instead of complain.*

. . . *go with the flow!*

Carry your written intention with you during the day, and check in with your intention and see if it helps you relax into the flow, especially when things are not going the way you thought they were "supposed" to go.

Practice

Establishing an Evening Ritual

Every evening, for at least thirty days, practice turning off anything that beeps, including your flat screen, at least two hours before you go to bed. Don't beat yourself up if you can't, just give it a try. You can even start with one hour and gradually build it up from there.

Take a minute to write down some of those unknown blessings from the morning that may have revealed themselves to you during the course of the day. Do this for thirty days and see how you feel. Then you can decide if you want to continue with this practice.

Today I was blessed by . . . *the smell of rain*

. . . *unexpected laughter.*

. . . *the opportunity to share a memory with someone who listened well.*

. . . *experiencing the fulfillment of my morning intention.*

The Art of Devotion

What makes a place sacred is the energy and intention brought to it. That is one of the reasons why churches, temples, art galleries, and nature can feel holy. In these places we often feel closer to Spirit and to the mystery of our true nature. People go to these places with the intention of praising. To praise is to express approval. Praise is an affectionate high-five and *yes* to beauty, mystery, and life!

- What do you praise in your life?
- Mountains, moon, nature, friendship, hugs,

honesty, laughter, ____________________,
____________________, ____________________,
____________________, ____________________,

- Where do you seek praise?
- Externally? Internally? ____________________,
____________________, ____________________,
____________________, ____________________,

Imagine being devoted to accepting and loving yourself unconditionally in this moment.

Imagine being devoted to discovering who you truly are.

- What does devotion look like to you?
- Being present, feeling connected, ____________,
____________________, ____________________,
____________________, ____________________,

Devotion practice takes time, space, and energy. Developing a devotional practice will change your life.

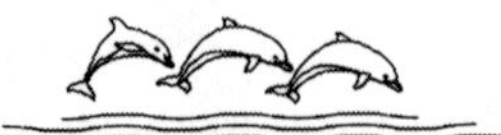

Practice

Setting Up an Altar

You may already have loads of altars all around your home and place of work; you just don't call them that yet. Unconsciously, we all naturally designate places to honor what is sacred to us. This may look like a framed picture of a beloved on your desk, a vase of fresh flowers on your dresser, a plant on your windowsill, a child's drawing on the fridge, a statue of a deity on your dashboard, or a favorite holiday photo on your screensaver. All of these examples invite you to pause and recognize what is sacred in your life. Friends, family, nature, spirituality, community—you name it.

Now let's bring this into consciousness. In your sacred space you can easily set up an "official" altar. You can do this on a window ledge, desk, or tabletop. It's nice to have a cloth of your choosing to lay your items upon.

What would you like to place on the altar of your heart?

I like to have something to represent the elements of earth, air, water, and fire. It's up to you but, as usual, here are some suggestions:

★ candle

★ incense

★ bowl of water

★ fresh flowers

★ rock or crystal

★ photos or statues of deities and/or beloveds

★ symbols representing your hopes, dreams, and longings

Be as simple or elaborate as you like. Make it inviting. It doesn't matter how fantastic it looks if you don't use it. The most important thing is that you *go* there. Going to the same place over and over again with the consistent intentions of resting, praising, and connecting to sacred space builds up energy over time and can have the same effect as charging a battery. Except this battery is your soul.

Practice

Creating Your Portable Pop-Up Altar

The first thing I do whenever I travel and stay in hotels or rentals is find a space to set up my altar. Once I have cleared a space and set up my altar, I can practice more easily and call it *home*.

For this practice you will need a piece of durable paper (watercolor paper works well), as you can paint and/or paste on it if you choose.

Take your paper and fold each side to meet at the middle. The paper should be able to stand freely. Now you have three panels on the front and three on the back that you can decorate with images and or words to create your very own pop-up altar.

You can place it in your sacred space, bring it to work, and take it on the road with you. It's a simple and creative way of designing your own altar and a reminder to take some time every day to connect with what is sacred to you.

Psst: have fun with this!

You Are Sacred

5

The Practice of Self-Love

Are you remembering to practice the principles from the first chapter? I hope so.

> *Reminder: Just for Today . . . I am my own* ***Compassionate Witness***

The role of witness invites us to take a step aside and observe the situation, without criticism and judgment. Many of us find this an easy and natural response when we encounter someone else giving herself a hard time. We can see that the person is suffering, and we are moved to do something to alleviate their pain. The feeling of compassion that has stirred in your heart inspires you to take action. It could be anything from listening, validating their feelings, offering another way to look at the situation, or giving them a hug.

However, when we give ourself a hard time, where does that compassionate impulse go? Do we listen to ourself without judgment? Give ourself a hug? Too often we don't—but we need to. Imagine being able to do this for yourself on a daily basis. Doing so effectively requires that you practice. Pay attention and notice when you start to beat yourself up with negative self-talk or self-defeating behavior. Be your own compassionate witness by taking an action to tend to your aching heart.

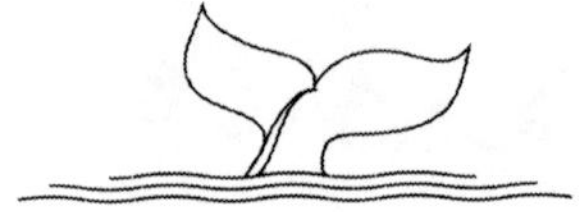

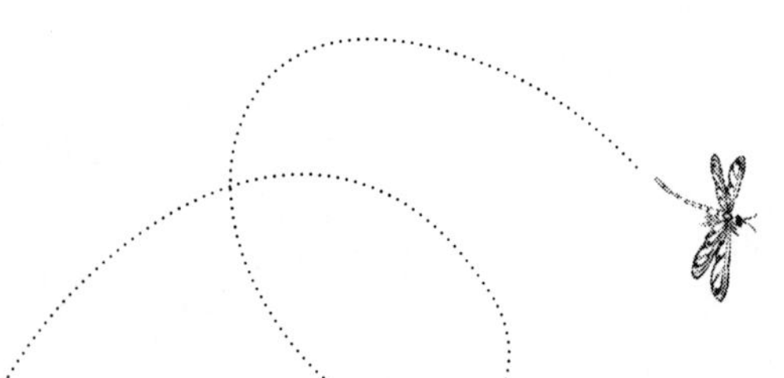

Treasure the Moments

Witnessing Your Heart

- *Right now, my heart feels* ______________________
  ____.

- *The last time my heart ached was* ______________
  ____.

- *The last time my heart sang was* ______________
  ____.

Remember that the heartache you experience is the beginning of an awakening in consciousness.

~ ANANDAMAYI MA

As a culture I don't think we pay enough attention to our hearts. Most of us only begin to notice them when they hurt or feel like they are breaking. What if those heartaches and hurts were there for the sole purpose of breaking our hearts open even wider? Would we begin to experience the unknown regions of our hearts, the spaces that are longing to be revealed?

Maybe breaking our hearts open is actually the *soul's purpose,* to help us connect with why we are here and what is waiting to be discovered. Many spiritual traditions advise that the soul resides behind the heart. If that is the case, then the cracks in your breaking heart are making room for your soul to shine through.

Imagine beginning to see your heartache as an opportunity to get curious about everything you do not know about your heart, instead of something painful to avoid and escape from.

I guarantee: if you are willing to enter into relationship with your own heart, your experience of life will *change*.

Map It

Milestones of Your Heart

❁ *Right now, my heart feels* ________________________,
and this reveals ________________________________
____
______________________________ *about my soul.*

❁ *The last time my heart ached was* __________________,
and this revealed ______________________________
____
______________________________ *about my soul.*

❁ *The last time my heart sang was* __________________,
and this revealed ______________________________
____
______________________________ *about my soul.*

Heart Chakra

Some of you may be familiar with the ancient Sanskrit term chakra, which means *energy center*. There are many chakras located throughout the body, but we are going to focus on the seven main ones, as outlined on the diagram.

Each chakra is related to a different part of the body that affects our organs and tissue, as well as our emotional and mental states. Many Eastern health systems (dating as far back as 5,000 years) maintain that in order for the physical, mental, and emotional body to be in a state of optimal health and wellness, all the chakras must be vibrating and rotating in a clockwise direction at the same rate. Disease (*dis*-ease) occurs when chakras get blocked or shut down. This can happen for a wide variety of reasons ranging from emotional, physical, and mental stresses, trauma, shock, disappointments—basically, life! The real or perceived harm may have long passed, but the energy centers in the body may not have gotten the message yet. That means some of the chakras may have slowed or shut down, resulting in you feeling sad, alone, tired, crappy, down, and generally out of balance.

Take a moment to connect with the energy center of your heart.

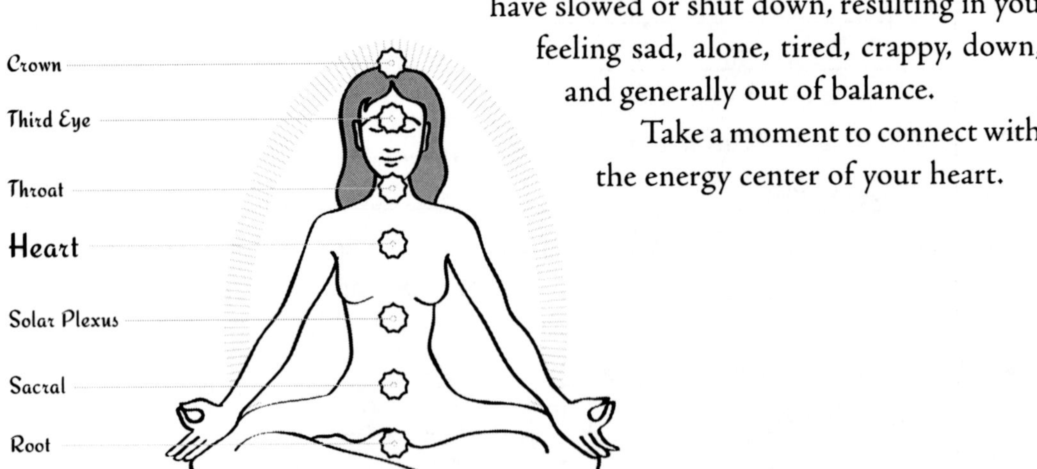

Practice

Energizing the Heart Chakra

Ponder these few things before we dive in—don't think too hard, just allow the answers to spontaneously arise in your heart:

- *In kindergarten, I wanted to grow up to be* _______ _______________________________________.
- *The three qualities I look for in a person are* ______ _______________________________________.
- _______________________________________ ___________________________ *lights up my heart.*
- _______________________________________ ___________________________ *breaks my heart.*
- _______________________________________ *is a quirky trait of mine that I love.*
- *For fun, I like to* ___________________________ _______________________________________.

The heart chakra is super-sensitive and does its best to stay open and help us receive and give love every day. However, as we have all experienced from time to time, when we get hurt, our natural tendency is to pull back. When we do this over an extended period of time, our heart chakra can get blocked or even shut down, which can disconnect us from our innocence, our childlike sense of wonder, our appreciation and "in-joy-ment" of life.

It can be difficult to discover the magnificence, vastness, and beauty of your own heart without first revealing the hurts that are lodged there.

Take your time with the following questions and just allow the answers and feelings associated with them to emerge.

- Who has hurt you in the past?
- Whom have you hurt in the past (unconsciously or consciously)?
- How do you feel when you think of these people?
- Are you willing to forgive yourself and the people who have hurt you?

Forgiveness

Forgiveness is not a one-time thing; forgiveness is a lifestyle.

~ Dr. Martin Luther King

Forgiveness is not a small thing. You may not feel ready to forgive *at this moment*. That is okay—for now. Before you use the word *never*, please consider forgiveness in the following context. It does not imply that the action that caused the hurt was okay. You can forgive *the person*, including yourself. **The act of forgiveness means that you are no longer willing to carry the pain around in your heart.** When you don't forgive, you are agreeing to clutter your heart with dis-ease that only hurts you in the end. When you forgive, you are saying to the universe: *I am giving You this hurt to take and transform. OPEN ME UP TO RECEIVE MORE LOVE, PLEASE!*

Where there is no love, put love—and you will find love.

~ SAINT JOHN OF THE CROSS

Ho'oponopono

In Hawaii there is an ancient, beautiful chant called *Ho'oponopono*. Originally it was sung by elders of a tribe to help reconcile and "to make right" when there was conflict among family or community members. It is now widely sung all around the world by anyone who wants to let go of hurt, bitterness, and resentment.

Literally translated it means: "I am sorry. Please forgive me. Thank you. I love you."

What I have realized while chanting this is that it doesn't matter if you are the one seeking or granting the forgiveness. The sounds and intentions carry their own powerful healing. Ultimately, you are forgiving yourself for having carried the burden of pain in your heart. I have often included chanting Ho'oponopono as a part of my daily meditation practice, calling to mind anyone or any situation that needs forgiving and healing. I can't explain how it works, it just does! You can put it to any tune or say it like a prayer or mantra.

There are many beautiful versions of this chant that you can find on YouTube. I like the version by my good friend and author Celeste Yacoboni, which you can check out on *CD Baby*.

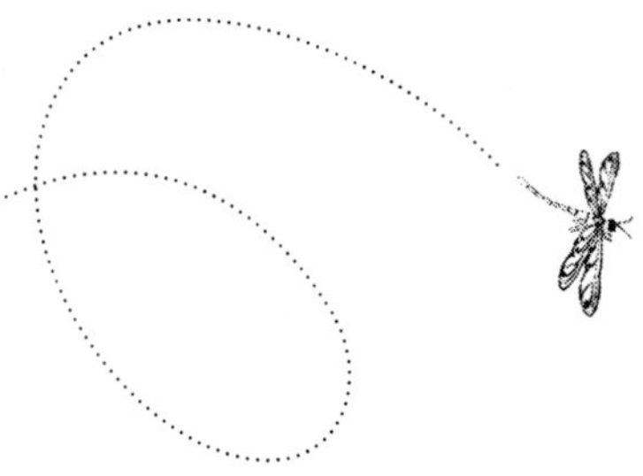

Practice

Ho'oponopno

The weak cannot forgive; forgiveness is a quality of the strong.

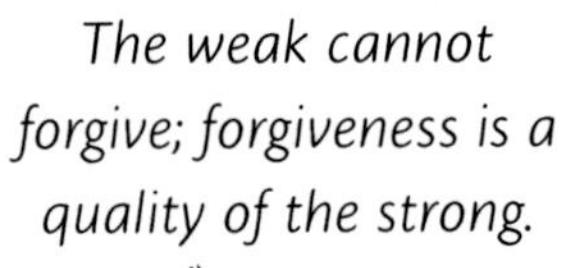

~ MAHATMA GANDHI

Ever experience a negative thought or story replaying over and over (and over) in your head? You know it is futile, a waste of time, a habit, and yet you can't stop it.

Try practicing this chant for a few minutes the next time that negative message starts. You can also use the English phrases. Take a breath, close your eyes, place your hands over your heart, and say any part of the chant to yourself, and notice what happens:

I am sorry. Please forgive me. I love you. Thank you.

You may discover a quiet joy, a light, a peace, something unknown that resides in your heart, just waiting for you to turn toward it. The Ho'oponopono practice invites us to dream a new dream, to tell a new story, instead of the familiar one replaying in our heads. Let this be a dream that supports your transformation and contributes to the dream of the whole community.

Practice this often, and rest there as long as you can.

Please be kind and patient with yourself during this process. Allow yourself to feel and experience anything that wants to be known to you. Let the anger and the tears flow, if they want to come—they are not coming up to give you a hard time, they are coming up to be healed. Those moist tears can help soften your heart and act like a river, bringing you somewhere new.

In my own practice, I sometimes imagine I am brought to a **garden of forgiveness**, where amazing growth happens.

Practice

Gardening

You can't force a rose to open. You can tend to it, though, and admire its beauty in every stage of its opening. Even more importantly, the plants that grow affect us, stimulating the spirit of growth within us. Hang out in the garden for a while and imagine how you would like it to nourish you.

- What needs tending to in your heart?
- What weeds need to be pulled?
- How deep do you need to go to dig up the roots?
- What kind of seeds do you want to plant in this garden?

A Caterpillar in Your Garden

As a species, history shows us that crisis usually precedes evolution. The caterpillar has no idea that it is going to turn into a beautiful butterfly one day. No clue that the colorful and majestic butterflies gleefully fluttering through the sky are its own destiny.

What the caterpillar calls the end of the world, the Master calls a butterfly.

~ Lao Tzu

We know that when the caterpillar reaches a certain point on its life journey, it starts producing "imaginal cells." These imaginal cells are so incredibly different from the cells it already produces that its immune system reacts in defense and starts attacking the new imaginal cells. The caterpillar is oblivious to the fact that these imaginal cells are Mother Nature's mysterious way of transforming the caterpillar into a unique and glorious butterfly. To the caterpillar, it must seem that its life as a caterpillar is being challenged and coming to an end. (It is!)

The caterpillar has no choice but to surrender his fate to these cells. Then, just when the caterpillar thinks it's all over: bang! New life bursts forth and he's now a butterfly. What a trip that must be!

Get where we are going here? Yep, it's a metaphor for your own journey.

Have faith in your imaginal cells. Imagine that your heart is full of them, swirling and coalescing. You can fight against them or get curious about them and co-create the next part of your life in collaboration *with* them. It's way more fun, I promise.

Whatever you can do or dream you can begin it now, for boldness has genius in it, power, and magic as well.

~ Johann Wolfgang von Goethe

Love without Shame

Along our journey toward self-love, we may encounter shame. Shame is like wearing a heavy, dark cloak throughout the summer. It may have been appropriate attire on a particular day or even for a season, but it is neither necessary nor healthy to keep wearing it once it has served its purpose.

What is the purpose of shame? To feel remorse over your actions and to feel how painful it is to be out of alignment with your higher self can often help you to pause before repeating the same behavior. Then it can be helpful. Feel it, make amends if possible, and let it go.

Yet in most cases, the only purpose shame serves is to keep your light and magnificence cloaked. This can be especially strong when we experience someone else's actions against us, when innocence has been violated, as in the case of abuse. When shame's only purpose is to stunt growth, it is like a disease, which if left untreated, slowly eats away at your heart and drains your spirit. The side effects are that you lose your ability to express yourself from your wise and innocent heart and to see yourself through clear and innocent eyes.

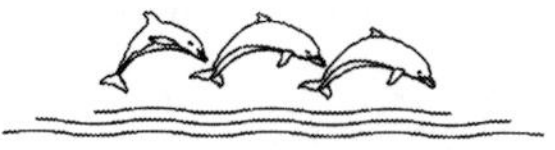

Practice

Being Shameless

Look in the mirror and repeat out loud, at least three times: ***"I love you without shame."***

Repeat it slowly and let the sound of your voice and the words fill the atmosphere. Stay with it. Notice how your heart feels. If tears come, let them. They will help soften, wash away, and release any shame lodged in your heart. Let the tears wash away shame and reveal what is there to be discovered.

I suggest repeating this practice often, for the rest of your life, if necessary. Be willing to approach it from a new place every day, letting go of any expectations and simply seeing what happens.

The Creative Power of Images

Why are images so powerful? An image can be a symbolic representation of what you *do not yet know.* It is an invitation to take a leap of faith into the unknown without having to figure anything out. Why limit yourself to your past experience of the world? There is so much beyond the edge of the known, just waiting for you.

Your relationships with images can take shape in a way you never could have dreamed. Images set the stage for you to have a creative relationship with what has *not yet* been revealed to you about yourself. *They are not explanations—they are possibilities.* Let pictures, symbols, colors, ideas, feelings, sounds, smells, or textures call out to you. Be drawn to them with intrigue, warmth, and curiosity. You may have no idea why you are choosing the pictures in the magazine, the fabric in the craft box, the piece of music, the leaf, the stone, the colors, but something in it calls to you. An image gets your attention in some way, and you respond by simply noticing.

Being creative is an act of expressing who we are, to ourselves first. That is where we start. So don't panic if you don't know who you are this moment. I guarantee: you are already so much more than you think.

Playtime!

Revealing Your Heart to Yourself Collage

Part I. One simple way to begin working with images is to get a big envelope or folder and some magazines. Allow a month to periodically go through the magazines, ripping out images (or words) that appeal to you or feel meaningful at the moment. Don't think too much or try to decide why you like something, just cut it out and put it in the folder. Trust that your selections have meaning.

Later, in Part II, you can assemble these pictures in relationship to each other in a collage, but for now—simply collect them. Think of it as a kind of visual diary that is totally personal to you. You can do this every day or every week and see how the images you are drawn to change over time.

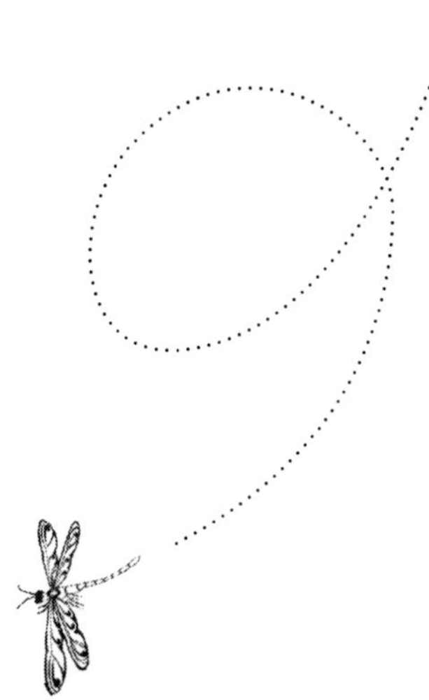

Part II. Set aside about one hour for this. Turn off your cell phone, email, and computer and put on some music you love. This is all about you.

To make your collage you'll need a bunch of magazines—or your folder of images—a poster-size sheet of paper, scissors, glue, and any other "bling" you like. Before you start, consciously give yourself permission not to have any idea of what your collage will look like. However, do take a moment to focus on the relationship you want to have with your heart and soul. Call to mind what you *want* instead of what you *don't want*. Thoughts create our experiences, and energy follows thought.

Quickly select any images that speak to you. Play with them, arrange them, wonder about them—and something you do not already know about yourself will start to emerge. This may be a feeling you can't explain, or it may be an aspect of your heart that you are just beginning to recognize. Trust these images. They want to reveal something to you. After a while it may feel as if the *images* are choosing *you*.

When you have all the images scattered around you, follow your intuition about where to place them on your paper. When you have finished, step back and see what your heart wants to show you.

Ellen's Story

Once upon a time, this world tried to break me. Making this collage inspires me to heal my past and embrace the unknown of my future. It shows me the home I have been searching for my whole life—the home in my heart. It had been there all along.

Debby's Story

I had never considered myself artistic and did not feel comfortable drawing, painting, or expressing myself in any artistic medium. I had not developed a sense of what I appreciated in art, style, or design. I was afraid to say I liked something if the people around me might not.

I signed up for Creative Discovery with no idea what to expect. From the beginning, Pasha gave us focus, inspiration, and—most importantly for me—permission to create freely and without judgment. I selected the elements of my project solely based on what appealed to me: colors, shapes, designs, textures—and I did not worry about the finished product. I let go of my fears and inhibitions. The creative process of the session allowed me to validate myself, please myself, and bear witness to my developing self.

Now, embracing my creativity is integral to my continued development, health, happiness, and well-being. My collage hangs on my bedroom wall, reminding me to live from my heart. It makes me feel warm, secure, and happy—feelings I desperately needed at that point in my recovery journey.

Journal Keeping: A Place to Speak to and from Your Heart

Many of you already are sold on the benefits of keeping a journal. Others have probably thought about it and intended to, yet have never gotten around to it. In our busy lives, it may be hard to take the time to write down private thoughts, dreams, musings, and experiences. A journal can be a life-saving friend when one is going through difficult times. It can be a place for you to work out feelings that perhaps you don't understand or cannot contain. Even if you share your inner life freely with a friend, partner, or other confidante in your life, still there are things that are complex and difficult to convey to others, especially if we don't understand them ourselves.

A journal can allow you to observe your day-to-day feelings, thoughts, and experiences as a continuum. The more you write, the richer you will find your journal—expressing secret and intimate aspects of your*self*, allowing a kind of conversation to happen. Keeping a journal is one of the most powerful tools for self-understanding and, indeed, for healing. The freer you can allow yourself to be with words, without having to "make sense" of what you write, the more access you will gain to parts of yourself that have never been expressed. You'll see the seeds of your creative and spiritual potential blossom.

Practice

Writing Your Feelings Honestly

When you did the *Softening the Gaze* meditation in "The Practice of Gratitude" chapter, what feelings and emotions emerged? Be honest, and use this as an opportunity to notice your positive feelings and release any negative ones, resisting the temptation to explain them away or over-analyze them.

Once you have read over what you wrote, get up, get a blank piece of paper, change your seat, and hand the pen over to your compassionate witness self. Now write. Notice any differences?

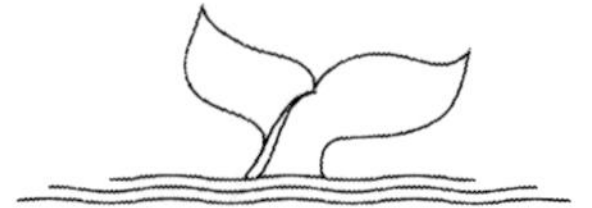

Treasure the Moments

Questions for Reflection and Journaling

- What do you long for?
- What is troubling your heart?
- What are you passionate about?
- What are some of your wildest dreams?
- Be bold! Be daring! Dream big! Name them without trying to figure out how they will happen!
- Imagine you are living one of your wildest dreams: What are you doing? How are you feeling? What are you wearing? Who is around you? Are you outside or inside? Describe it in detail, noticing any sounds, smells, colors, and textures.

The Journey of Self-love

For over ten years I have kept the following story in my journal. On my journey, it is a signpost that guides my progress. I want to share it with you.

A Healer Told Me . . .

~ UNATTRIBUTED

"The longest distance you will ever travel is the path from your mind to your heart. You must practice losing your mind, she said—the old mind.

This old mind holds on so tight to figuring things out, controlling outcomes—pays so much attention to the spoilers of courage and creativity, the dark energy that haunts you underground, aims to trip you up, undermines you, paralyzes you with worry and fear.

You must transform that fear to LOVE. Only then will you meet the magic of your heart, articulate your bio-intelligence, feel your deep compassion, ignite your sensual knowing.

Only then will you live your true purpose, speak your own language, tell your true story. If you do this, life can become truly amazing.

If you dare yourself, keep the energy moving, ingest more sunshine, find the drumming, singing, and dancing—the sensuality of your heart and your passion—you will break through and change the pattern.

There are many helpers available to you. Ask them to guide your journey and to help you clear the path from the mind to the heart."

Imagine the unknown is *LOVE.*

I do not trust people who don't love themselves and yet tell me, "I love you." There is an African saying, which is: Be careful when a naked person offers you a shirt.

~ MAYA ANGELOU

The Spiritual Practice of Loving Yourself

When you LOVE yourself, you can love others—for real.

Loving oneself often gets a bad rap. It can be associated with being egotistical and selfish. (Usually, people who accuse others of these things don't love themselves.) When you love and accept yourself from your heart, you see everyone as a reflection of that love, and therefore a reflection of yourself.

Love does not come from a place of thinking and insecurity, generated by the mind. It comes from the light shining through the cracks in your heart.

Love is an attitude. It's also a lifestyle, though few people will congratulate you on caring and tending to your heart. How often have you heard, "Way to go on that self-care and self-love!"?

You have to go toward it, not expecting any accolades from anyone. In fact, as you change your attitude and lifestyle, people who say they love you may get nervous, plant seeds of doubt in your mind, and accuse you of all sorts of selfish behavior. Don't get defensive—the heart doesn't defend, only the ego does. Send them love and keep going.

What are some of the things you are doing to shift this principle of self-love from a concept to your direct experience?

How do you imagine you can practice being an even better compassionate witness to yourself?

Practice

Writing a Love Letter to Yourself

Can you imagine what it would look like to enter into a kinder and softer relationship with yourself? Imagine you are a person in love with yourself right now—not *when* or *if only*. Just for today, imagine the kind of relationship you could have with yourself if you loved and valued yourself now.

I invite you to sit down and write yourself a "love letter." Don't over-think it, just sit down and write. Give yourself fifteen minutes. Don't lift your hand from the page. Write with reckless abandon. Go!

Now place it in an envelope, seal it, and mail it to yourself. This is an important part of the process. Mail it and see what it feels like to receive it. No one else ever has to see it. Write from your heart, from your soul. This could be the most powerful and loving gift you give to yourself. I have done this at different times in my life, and I keep my love letters close to me. I re-read them, to remind myself when I forget.

Affirmation:

"I am loved, loving, and loveable, right now."

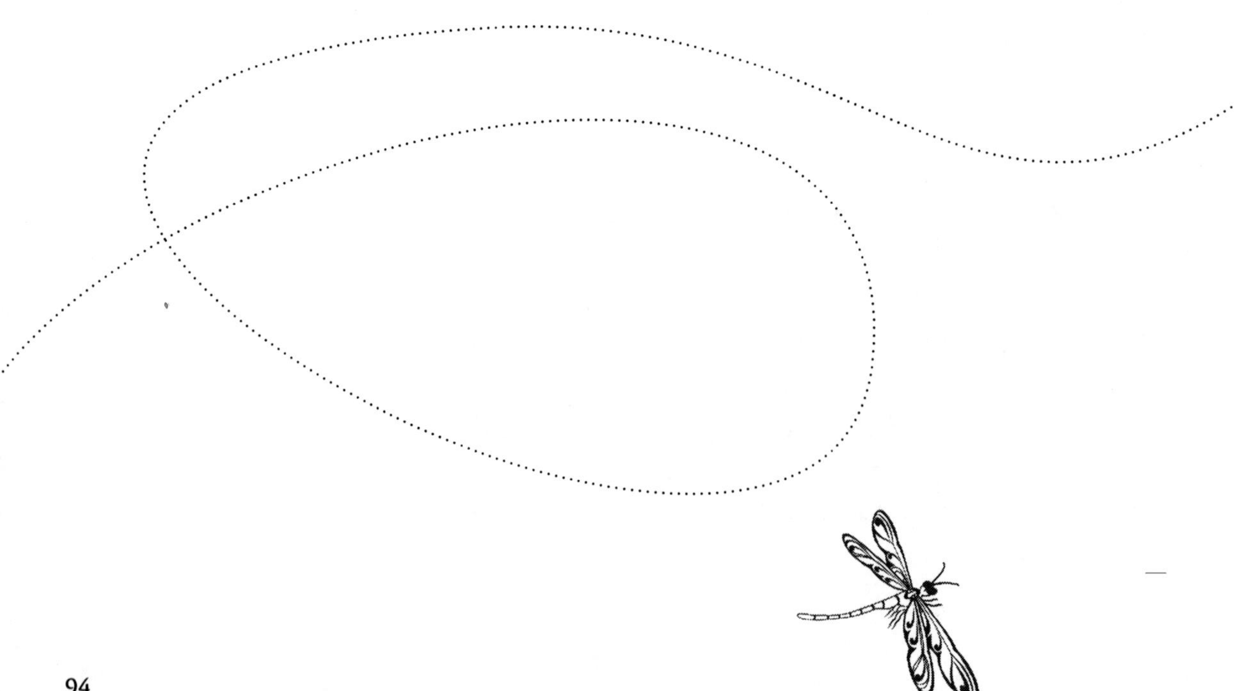

6

The Practice of Happiness

Happiness is a responsibility. It is something we all crave, yet few of us see it as something that requires time to cultivate and turn our attention and energy toward. For some strange reason we think we are entitled to it. When this expectation of ready-made happiness is not met, it is common for feelings of judgment, low self-esteem, and depression to rise to the surface and take over.

You have to want it to go after it!

One way to attain happiness is to find ways to practice it.

Happiness is not something ready made. It comes from your own actions.

~ Dali Lama

Treasure the Moments

What Do You Believe Makes You Happy?

Uncensored. Go!

1. ______________________________

____

We hold these truths to be self-evident: that all men are created equal, that they are endowed by their Creator with certain unalienable rights, that among these are life, liberty, and the pursuit of happiness.

~ Thomas Jefferson (The Declaration of Independence)

2. ____

____

3. ____

____

4. ____

____

5. ____

____

I have asked hundreds of people this question in workshops. The answers include being in nature, playing with kids, walking the dog, cooking, eating a great meal, laughing with friends, toast, and feeling heard and understood. No one has ever said money. Not one.

When I reflect this back to the groups, most of them are surprised. Are you? As a culture we say we want to be happy, but we are preoccupied with the pursuit of money instead, and we wonder why we are not happy. Yes, we need money to survive, but how much do we really need? When I was working my way up the corporate ladder, a ladder that has no end, I found out firsthand that the amount of money I made bore little relationship to the amount of happiness I was experiencing. My "mantra" during that time was "work hard, play hard." It brought me to my knees. Not out of devotion but out of stress and exhaustion.

Practice

Shopping

Next time you are shopping, stop and ask yourself: will this purchase make me happy?

Although this is a one-question practice, it is challenging. We are deeply programmed to think that more possessions make us more important, desirable, smart, successful, and so on. Often we accumulate stuff to cover up how we feel about ourselves. I know. I have acquired many pairs of shoes over the years. Each one of them made me happy, for a very short period of time.

Usually, we are happy when we get what we want or achieve a goal we have set. But as soon as circumstances change or we set another goal or desire, the feeling of happiness subsides or passes. You may think that achieving the goal or getting the thing makes you happy. It doesn't. **You are happy because your mind is in your heart.**

Robert Adams, the late meditation teacher and devotee of the great Indian saint Sri Ramana Maharshi (who gave us the great question, "Who am I?") illustrates this beautifully in one of his talks which is summarized here as follows:

Mind in the heart (thoughts still and peaceful) = Happiness

Mind outside the heart (thoughts always changing) = victim of thoughts = Not Happy

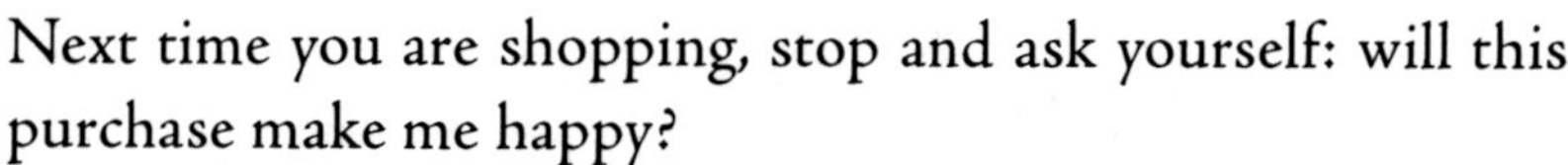

It is up to you. You decide how happy you are going to be by how much time you devote to experiences that create happiness. As a concept, it really is that simple. As a practice, cultivating happiness is something that requires discipline and dedication.

Practice

When Is Your Mind Most Likely to Be in Your Heart?

Example: My mind is outside my heart when *I'm scheming, comparing, judging.*

My mind is outside my heart when ________________
____.

Example: My mind is inside my heart when I'm *allowing, accepting, forgiving.*

My mind is inside my heart when ________________
____.

Develop this further by examining ways you can bring your mind into your heart—even for mundane chores like shopping or cleaning.

Self-esteem vs. Other-esteem

Running after happiness, as if it were something outside to grab, or thinking you have to be happy all the time are sure-fire ways to be miserable. Often we think "shoulds" will make us happy, but they don't.

No "other" can make you happy; yet, no man is an island. We need each other to procreate, create, thrive, and grow. We easily get into trouble, though, when we derive our sense of self from another person, activity, or substance. For example: Cheryl thinks she is important because she is married to Joe. Jack thinks he has it made, as he plays golf every Saturday with his friends. Susan shops online and is addicted to accumulating friends on social media sites. Mark is addicted to porn. Annie feels like she is the life of the party after a few glasses of wine and everyone laughs at her jokes. Scott is happiest when he has a pretty girlfriend.

Does how you feel about yourself ever change depending on the presence or absence of a particular person, activity, or substance?

As humans we are wired to seek people and situations to make us feel good; it is part of the human experience. And there is nothing wrong with it, except when that is how we identify or define ourselves: in relation to "other"—when we only feel good or happy when that other tells us we are good, or they need us, or we need them to feel happy. When your experience of yourself is determined by how someone else reacts to you, it's a setup for disappointment.

What happens when the "other" doesn't show up or say what you want to hear? Inevitably, unhappiness.

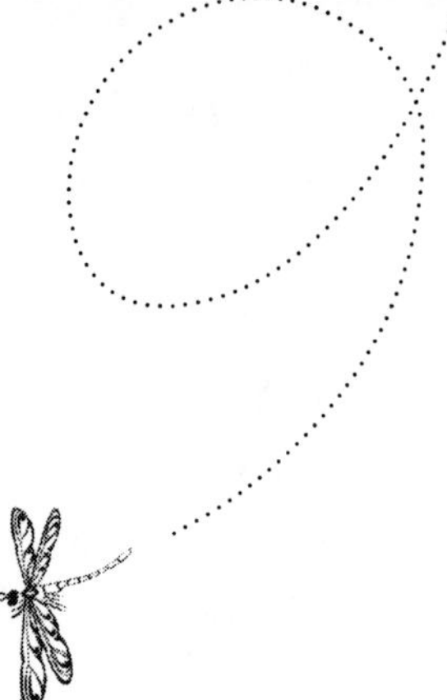

Practice

Cultivating Happiness

This isn't rocket science—you can do it!

1. **Notice**

Slow down! Stop taking everyday interactions with important strangers for granted. For example, look at the face of the person who is giving you change at the tollbooth, serving you coffee, or greeting you in the elevator. Recognize that person as someone who, just like you, wants to experience happiness today.

Practice smiling more.

That goes for people you live and work with, too, not just important strangers!

Notice everything. Live in wonder. Open your eyes.

Breathe mindfully.

Smiling is the highest form of meditation.

~ AMMA

2. **Connect**

These days we spend so much time in front of computer screens and electronic devices. I am sure I am not the first person to wonder: how *social* is social media?

It is fantastic that we can stay in touch with people across the world in real time. What about actually being within "touching distance" with the friend across town or across the street?

Research shows that people who regularly get together with friends and family are generally happier than people who don't. Human beings crave connection with each other. It is just the way we are made. It doesn't imply that you are needy or can't bear to be alone. It indicates that you have a heart that loves to give and receive love.

How often do you spend time with friends in a social setting?

If the answer is "not enough" or "I don't have time," I suggest you make the necessary changes to reschedule and reprioritize. Happiness is worth the effort. Take the initiative, reach out, and suggest meeting a friend for lunch or dinner. Say yes to the next invitation you receive.

If you don't have friends in your area, or they believe they are too busy, get out of your comfort zone and make some new ones. Join a dance class, hiking club, cooking or painting workshop. Let it be something you enjoy doing, or always wanted to do, and share the experience.

Beginning today, treat everyone you meet as if they were going to be dead by midnight. Extend to them all the care, kindness, and understanding you can muster, and do it with no thought of any reward. Your life will never be the same again.

~ Og Mandino

3. Serve – Compassion in Action

In the yogic tradition there is the term *seva*. It refers to serving selflessly, meaning you do it with no expectation of getting something out of it for yourself. You serve irrespective of praise or blame, just because you are able to.

I don't know what your destiny will be, but one thing I know: the only ones among you who will be really happy are those who have sought and found how to serve.

~ Albert Schweitzer

Helping out is not some special skill. It is not the domain of rare individuals. It is not confined to a single part of our lives. We simply heed the call of that natural impulse within and follow where it leads us.

~ Ram Das

How wonderful it is that nobody need wait a single moment before starting to improve the world.

~ Anne Frank

I have often approached service with this attitude, only to find that I was attached to getting something out of it, like recognition. When the sincere outpourings of gratitude came, it often pumped up my ego and made me feel good, for a short time. Conversely, on the few occasions where indifference was expressed, or even resentment toward the help offered, I experienced feelings of disappointment, anger, and withdrawal—not in alignment with the yogic philosophy of service, perhaps, but certainly in alignment with the human and wounded part of me.

Even though I am aware of this dance with my ego regarding service, it still comes up. Now, instead of backing away from it and feeling bad about myself, I see it as an opportunity to practice how to serve more. Ultimately, I am practicing yoga, in a way that feels meaningful.

When we can get out of our minds and serve from our hearts, not wanting anything in return, something beautiful and unexpected happens. Grace comes in, and with that happiness.

How can you serve more?

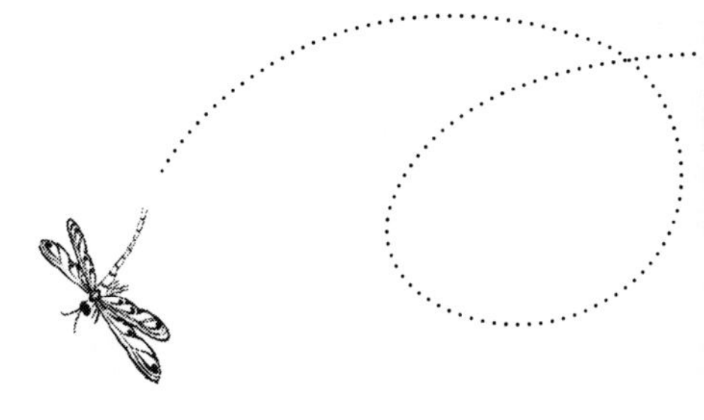

Practice

Brainstorming 9-Ways-to-Serve

Start out by writing down activities that bring you alive. If you come up with nine, great; if not, no worries. All you need to get started is one.

- ______________________________ *brings me alive.*
- ______________________________ *brings me alive.*
- ______________________________ *brings me alive.*
- ______________________________ *brings me alive.*
- ______________________________ *brings me alive.*
- ______________________________ *brings me alive.*
- ______________________________ *brings me alive.*
- ______________________________ *brings me alive.*

Don't ask yourself what the world needs. Ask yourself what makes you come alive and then do that. Because what the world needs is people who have come alive.

~ HOWARD THURMAN

In this life we cannot do great things. We can only do small things with great love.

~ MOTHER THERESA

Yes, the world needs your help, but saving the world is a daunting task. Overwhelm quickly sets in and the "thinking mind" tells us that what we do won't make a difference. So we end up doing nothing.

You can start by choosing one place to donate your time, or pick a few before you make a commitment to one. The key is to make a commitment to serve and follow through with it. Promise yourself you will donate a particular amount of time each month, show up with no expectation of getting anything, and see how it feels to simply serve.

For example, you may want to help prepare food at a homeless shelter or lend a hand at an animal shelter. You could get involved with an adult literacy program if that resonates with you, donate your time at a community garden, or read to folks at a nursing home. You may know someone who could use some help with kids after school or with walking dogs in the morning. The list is endless. Have fun with it and get creative!

I slept and I dreamed that life is all joy. I woke and I saw that life is all service. I served and I saw that service is joy.

~ KAHLIL GIBRAN

4. **Move!**

Get up off the coach and get your energy flowing.

Walk every day, or at least five days a week. Do it for the joy and nothing else. If you find it hard to do it by yourself, invite a friend to join you. Turn it into a happiness practice instead of a chore, and notice the difference.

"Dance like you need the money!" (I saw this on a bumper sticker in Santa Fe and loved it.) To get motivated you can try putting on Pharrell Williams's *Happy* video on YouTube (or any music you like). I did this first thing every morning for one week as an experiment, and it transformed my day.

Yoga is a beautiful practice to keep you in your heart while moving.

The term *yoga* has been in use for over 5,000 years. According to the ancient and sacred Indian text, the *Bhagavad Gita*, yoga is about doing our duty to the best of our ability and abandoning all attachment to success and failure. Basically, just do your best and don't worry about the results.

Imagine it is your duty to be happy. Find your yoga. Practice and let go!

You can find a class and teacher in your area that are in alignment with your intention by doing a little research online, or you can ask for a recommendation at your local health food store or community center. There are also many DVDs and online classes to choose from. You can always check out my yoga DVD offering, *Yoga: New Beginnings*, which is available on my website and includes a morning and evening practice to get you started. Please do not be intimidated if you are new to yoga. There is so much more to yoga than twisting your body into all kinds of shapes. There is a place for everyone to enter; it is up to you to find that place and roll out a mat.

Yoga is also defined as moving from one point to a higher point. Movement requires change. One of the biggest things you can change with a consistent yoga practice is the relationship you have with yourself.

Be happy. It's one way of being wise.

~ Sidonie-Gabrielle Colette

5. Relax

For many of us change, even when it is positive, implies stress. Moving from your comfort zone into your discovery zone can be stressful.

Let's return to the stress-busting practice in the chapter on creating sacred space. Do that practice again, and then ask yourself these questions:

- *What does relaxing look like to you?*
- *Do you set aside some time to rest every day?*
- *How do you feel when you do "nothing"?*
- *What are you afraid you may discover if you slow down?*
- *What are some of the stories about relaxing that you carry? Do any of them include some of the following words or expressions?*

just an excuse to be lazy . . .
there is no time . . .
not productive . . .
a luxury . . .
can't sit still . . .
afraid of losing control . . .
too difficult . . .
things will fall apart if I stop . . .
it's boring . . .
too much to do . . .

What if you didn't take all the stories you tell yourself for granted?

What if you didn't believe every thought?

Don't wait for life to force you to slow down. One day, when you are least expecting it, it will.

Remember: all stress isn't bad. Sometimes when great things are in the process of happening, we can experience high levels of stress. Promotions in work, planning vacations, new love relationships, careers, and moving to a new location all have the potential to cause anxiety. The factor that most stress-inducing thoughts have in common is CHANGE. We explored our comfort zones in the chapter on the practice of not knowing. Let's go a little deeper into the origins of our comfort zone:

❀ How did you cope with change as a child?

- Were you advised of changes taking place in the home?

- How did your caretakers deal with stress?

- Did you trust the adults in your life to be able to take care of you in the midst of transitions?

Do any of your answers bear a relationship to how you deal with stressful situations today? We often unconsciously carry our early childhood experiences and habits into adulthood without questioning where they came from. Once we begin to notice the patterns and cycles we engage in, we can have a relationship with them.

Is it a relationship that works for you, or is it a relationship that needs some tending?

Imagine changing a stress reaction into a relaxation response.

Psst:
Slow down your breathing.

Practice

Stress-busting

Notice when the stressful thoughts start to rise.

1. Interrupt them straightaway with a breath.
2. All you need is one tiny empty space that you can turn toward and then call in an action to center yourself.
3. The action can be in the form of taking another breath and repeating a positive affirmation, such as "All is well." "I am ok." "I am safe." "I am loved, loving, and loveable." "I am capable." "I am strong." "I am enough." "I am courageous." "I am connected."

Write 9 of your own affirmations (in the present tense) so you will have them at hand when you need them.

1. ______________________________________

   ____

2. ______________________________________

   ____

3. ______________________________________

   ____

4. ______________________________
____

5. ______________________________
____

6. ______________________________
____

7. ______________________________
____

8. ______________________________
____

9. ______________________________
____

The more you practice this before you are feeling stressed out, the more likely you are to remember to practice when you are in a stressful situation.

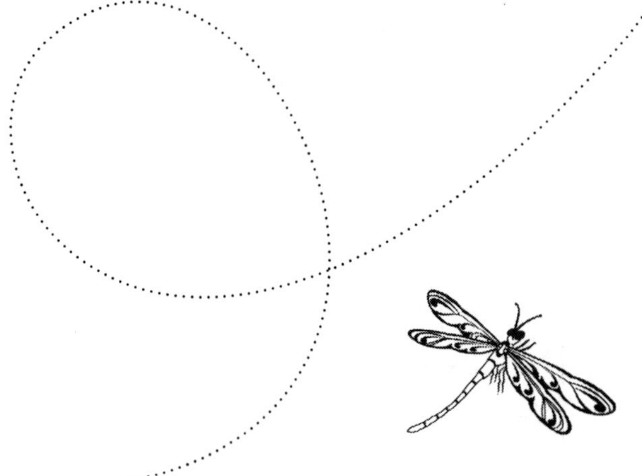

The Practice of Resting

Developing a Meditation Practice

You should sit in meditation for twenty minutes a day, unless you're too busy; then you should sit for an hour.

~ Old Zen Saying

What if you could develop a practice of simply not going against yourself?

One word we can use to describe that practice is *meditation*. Meditation is about turning down the volume of the internal critic and getting off your own back.

The word *meditation* can often be charged for people, who think they can't meditate. Let's demystify meditation. It is not reserved for "spiritual" people. If you can breathe, you can meditate. I promise.

Most of us can rest, from time to time, so let's just call it resting. After all, resting also is the practice of getting off our own backs and relaxing our hearts and minds.

When I decided I wanted to learn how to meditate, nearly twenty years ago, the first thing I noticed was how much time I spent talking to myself. It was quite startling at first. The more I told the thoughts to go away, the faster and stronger they came. After struggling through a few meditation instruction classes, I gave up. Everyone else in the class appeared to be so peaceful and relaxed. I was certain my mind was the only one that was totally freaking out and doing its own thing.

Every time I sat down with the intention of meditating, I beat myself up with the habitual negative self-talk I was so used to hearing. I declared myself a failure. So I forgot all about meditating and continued on with the very busy lifestyle I had gotten used to—until life showed up, in the form of a third cancer diagnosis, and forced me to take another look.

What I have discovered since is that *everybody's* mind is prone to behaving like an out-of-control racehorse. It is just what the mind does. It is the nature of the mind to judge, criticize, compare, mumble, shout, and seduce us with anything that is going to take us out of the present moment. However, the beauty of the mind is that we can notice when that happens and interrupt it with a practice.

The "practice" of resting is one powerful tool we can use to stop fighting with ourselves and cease struggling with circumstances, emotions, or moods. It is not about accomplishing anything and it is not a self-improvement course. It is not about winning or getting it right. What it *is* about is turning down the internal noise volume, relaxing into the present moment, and developing an attitude of acceptance and peace that can spread from our heart into the rest of our day and life.

We use the word *practice* because that is exactly what it is: the practice of replacing habits of a lifetime—and it takes time. Practice noticing the unruly thoughts for what they are and stop taking them so seriously. From now on it is your job to *notice*. By simply noticing, you can make a conscious decision to expose the endless stream of commentary and begin to claim peace, joy, and love.

When you start to practice anything new, it can seem like an impossible task. It is not easy to stop a running train at full speed! That is what your mind is. You don't start fighting with the train or your mind—you will never win. You practice getting out of the way and just watch it speed by. After some practice, watching the train (thoughts) becomes less interesting than watching your breath.

To name a thing
is to tame it.

~ CHINESE PROVERB

Resting is truly about nurturing ourself in the present moment and cultivating compassion and kindness toward our heart and mind. Our thoughts create our state of mind. Energy follows thought. When we rest, our mind follows our breathing. Our breath is the key. Our breath leads the way.

You can create space around your thoughts, which leads to creating sacred space in your body and your life. Where there is space, there is possibility.

Why Do This Practice?

- We meditate so we can relax.
- We meditate so we can discover who we truly are.
- We meditate to experience love in its purest form.
- We meditate to experience the infinite wonder of being alive.
- We meditate to help us rest in the unknown.

A relaxed mind is
a creative mind.

~ UNATTRIBUTED

One of the great contemporary spiritual teachers, Eckhart Tolle, tells us that meditation is about making the present moment your friend. I love that. The present moment is life. If you are experiencing this moment, you are alive. Meditation is life (you) experiencing life (all that is). Pretty cool stuff!

How Can You Practice This?

Resting can look like different things to each of us. It is the same with mediation. Meditation is all about the breath. You already know how to breathe. That implies to me that **you already know how to meditate**, and that you are probably doing some form of a meditation practice already—whether you know it or not. It could look like making art, swimming laps, cooking dinner, gardening, or any other activity that requires you to rest your racing mind and focus on the task at hand.

In my experience, it is helpful to have a technique or form to start off with, and then stick with that for a while so it doesn't seem so overwhelming at the beginning.

Once you get habituated to placing your mind in your heart (see the previous chapter), you can personalize it and bring it anywhere with you.

Guidelines to Help Cultivate a Mindful Meditation Practice

There are two parts to developing a resting practice:

1. Getting used to experiencing the practice of sitting in your body on a regular basis. This can be sitting cross-legged on the floor, in a chair with feet touching the floor, or lying down. If lying down, have your knees bent, if possible, so that your feet are connected to a flat surface. This will help ground you and keep you more present.

2. Carrying this experience around with you throughout your day. Once you have developed the habit, it is easier to call it to mind in stressful situations to help you relax wherever you are.

Part 1: Three Steps to Get Used to the Experience

Step One: Notice Your Body

Notice how your body feels. Check in with your shoulders, back, neck, facial muscles, and hands. Become aware of your body and make a choice to get into a kinder relationship with it while sitting. It is important to have a straight spine and an open heart, as this will help you stay alert and allow the breath and energy to flow. Choose comfort over form, though, or you won't sit for long!

Your eyes can be closed or lowered. The theory behind lowering them is that it helps keep you more present.

Step Two: Notice Your Breath

Breathe in through your nose, if you can, and follow the breath down to your throat, chest, and belly.

Ideally, we want our breath to go all the way down to three finger widths below the navel.

- It can help to visualize a full moon that is held in the cradle of your pelvis. Breathe into the moon and back up again.

Step Three: Get Comfortable with Technique

As you are breathing, what do you notice about your breath? Is it getting stuck anywhere?

Wherever you may be feeling tight or stuck, visualize that area being caressed by a warm and soothing breath.

Really feel the breath in your whole body. Is there discomfort anywhere in your body? Our tendency is to get away from it. I encourage you to breathe into the discomfort with warmth and kindness.

Practice this for as long as you can. There is no need to be uncomfortable for a long time. It is a practice that can lovingly be cultivated over time.

Honor yourself for taking time to develop a kinder relationship with your heart and mind. If the first day you sit down for one minute and the next time it's two minutes, celebrate yourself and start again tomorrow. Remember, this is a practice of not beating yourself up. I suggest slowly building up your sitting practice to twenty minutes, honoring your practice every breath of the way.

Practice

Morning Meditation

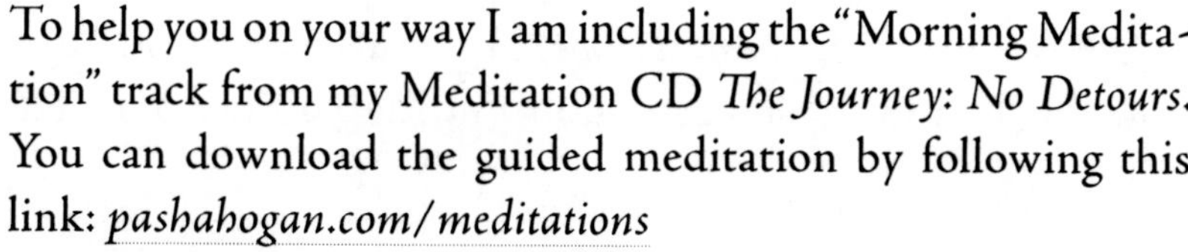

To help you on your way I am including the "Morning Meditation" track from my Meditation CD *The Journey: No Detours*. You can download the guided meditation by following this link: *pashahogan.com/meditations*

Remember, there is no way you can do this incorrectly. Developing a formal meditation practice takes time. It can be frustrating at first, and the temptation will be to declare you can't meditate and throw in the towel. Don't despair! You are not alone in that thinking. Just put it down, come back to it again, and start fresh.

This could be a good time to review practices from the first chapter on "The Practice of Beginning."

Be willing to be a beginner every single morning.

~ Meister Eckhart

Part 2: Carry the Practice with You

Whenever you find yourself in a stressful situation, you can take a couple of deep breaths and consciously invite warmth and kindness to flood your body. Your body is becoming habituated with the warm and kind breath to relax your mind.

Getting to know your hooks and triggers will help you notice when you are most likely to get carried away by your anxious and stress-inducing thoughts. When you feel yourself getting anxious, you can come back to your breath and interrupt the thought process with a friendly breath.

Psst: If you are having a hard time focusing on your breath, you can try counting breaths. Count down from the number ten on your exhale, like this:

- Exhale, inhale – ten
- Exhale, inhale – nine . . . and so on until one.

When you reach the number one, begin the count again, this time on the inhale, counting up from the number one, like this:

- Inhale, exhale – one
- Inhale, exhale – two . . . and so on until ten.

If you get distracted and lose your place, no big deal, just start again and keep going. You can repeat this cycle for as long as you need to.

This technique may not work for everyone, but it can be a good place to start if you don't already have a practice.

Adapt the practice so it works for you!

The most important thing is that you find a way that allows your breath to lead the way instead of your powerful thoughts and emotions.

Playtime!

Make Your Own Mala or Happiness Necklace

Mala is a Sanskrit word meaning "garland" or "wreath." *Bead*, an English word, derives from the Dutch noun *bede*, which means a "prayer."

Malas, or prayer beads, are used by various spiritual traditions all over the world to help count the number of prayers spoken or chanted.

Missionaries saw mala beads being used in the East and liked them so much they brought them back to the West and adapted them to create rosary beads, which are used for prayer in Catholicism.

Here we are going to play with this concept so you can use them as part of your resting practice if you choose. You can create a non-denominational set of beads that will help keep your mind focused on each breath or internally whisper one of your positive affirmations to keep you focused and in the moment.

Each mala consists of 108 beads, a sacred number, plus one additional bead, traditionally known as the *guru bead* or *teacher bead*. The 109th bead reminds us to pause to acknowledge and thank all of our teachers.

To make your own set of beads to help keep your mind focused in your heart, leading to more lasting and deeper happiness, you will need:

Basic Materials:

- ★ 108 similarly sized beads
- ★ One different bead
- ★ Piece of flexi-wire: length depends on how big the beads are

You can make your own set of beads by simply:

1. Stringing the 108 beads in a row followed by the slightly different bead.
2. Tying a secure knot to keep them in place. If you have access to jewelry-making tools, such as a crimper, you will be able to secure a better connection with the two ends of the flexi-wire. You can always visit your craft or bead store to help you with finishing it off.

Once the beads are strung together and the ends are closed off, you are all set!

Suggestions on how to use:

Starting with the first of the 108 beads and moving in a clockwise direction, finger each bead while internally reciting either your chosen affirmation or word. Alternatively, you can simply and consciously take one breath cycle (inhale and exhale) at each bead before moving on to the next one.

After doing one round, touching each of the 108 beads, pause and give thanks for your teachers, your breath, your life, your Higher Power, etc., and without touching or crossing over the 109th bead, flip the beads over and go back around in a counterclockwise direction. Do this as many times as you like.

When your mind strays, don't sweat it; just pull it back to your breath and your heart. Relax—you can't make a mistake! The point is that you are consciously choosing to take some time to be with your breath and your heart.

If you choose to wear your beautiful creation, you can always interrupt stressful thoughts from taking over by simply reaching for a bead and refocusing your mind on what supports you.

This can be a lovely way to start and finish each day. Enjoy!

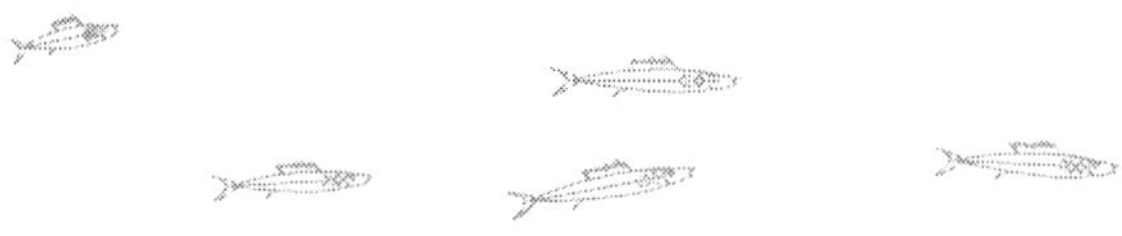

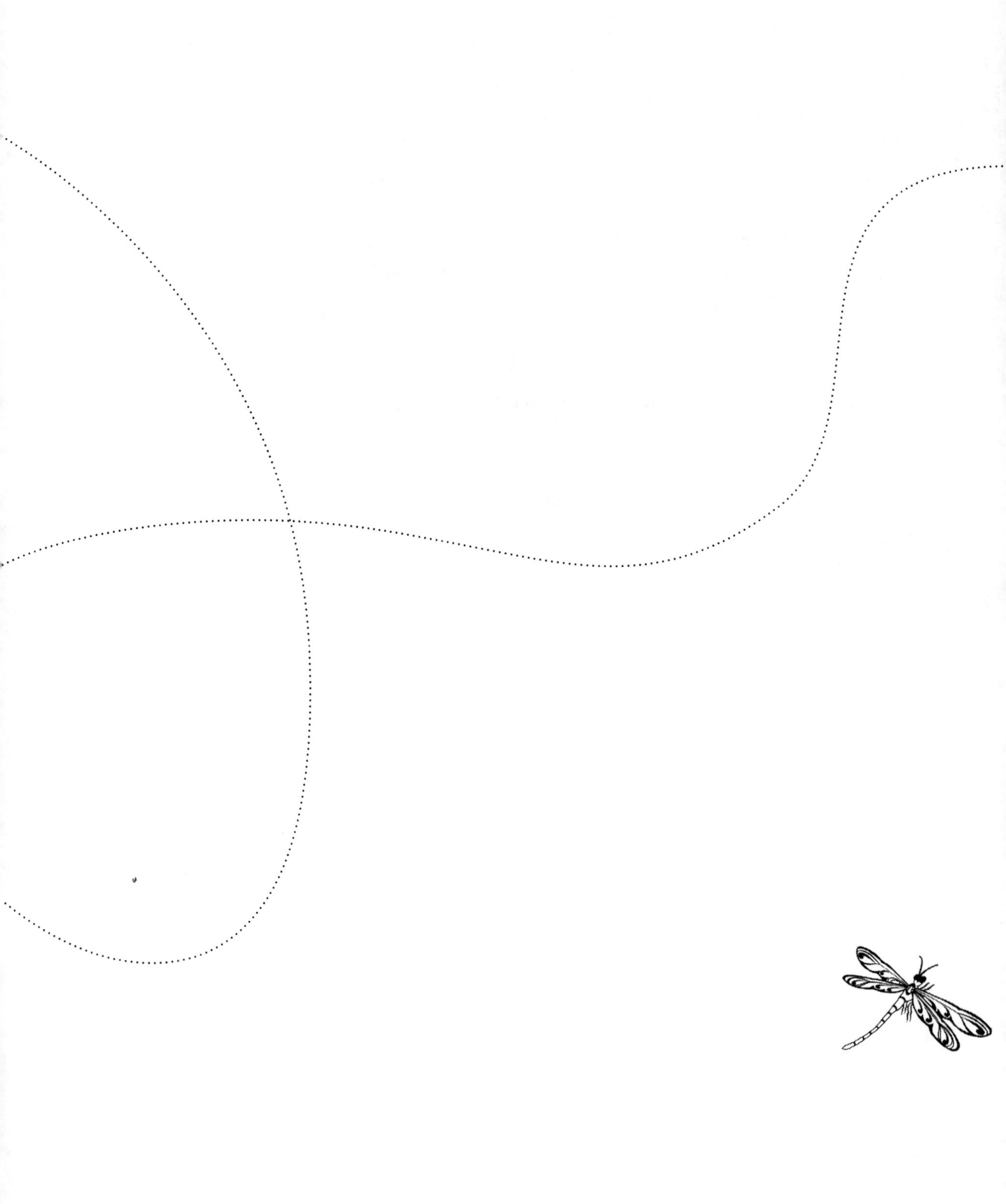

8

The Practice of Medicine

In most Western cultures, when we are not feeling well, we go to the doctor, get a prescription of sorts, and hope it will cure us. We place our faith in a cure in something or someone outside of ourselves and hope for the best. This chapter invites you to reexamine your relationship to medicine and what part you can play in writing your own prescriptions.

It doesn't interest me
what you do for a living.

I want to know what
you ache for,

And if you dare to
dream of meeting
your heart's longing.

~ ORIAH MOUNTAIN DREAMER

Most indigenous cultures distinguish *cure* vs. *healing*. A cure has a beginning and an end; healing is a multidimensional process. Someone can be cured but not healed. Healing is "medicine," and according to many facets of Native American wisdom, medicine is anything that connects us to the Great Mystery and all of life, which includes the healing of body, mind, and spirit. You can substitute for "Great Mystery" whatever word or phrase works for you: God/dess, Divine, Spirit, Higher Power, etc. In this context medicine is anything that connects you to unconditional love and brings your soul to life!

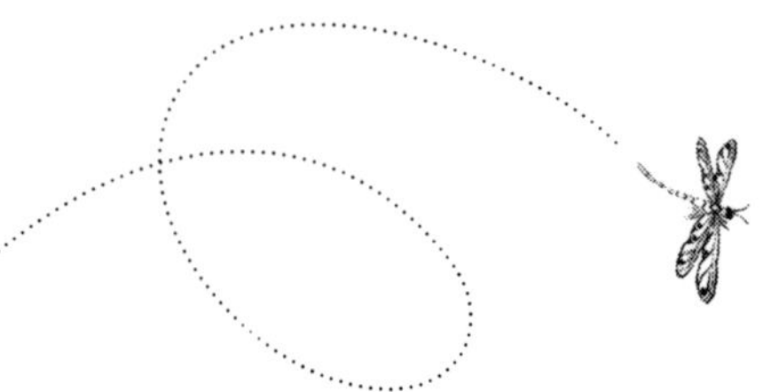

Treasure the Moments

What Is Your Medicine?

a. What feeds your soul, spirit, and heart? No censoring—go!

1. ______________________________
______________________________ *feeds me.*

2. ______________________________
______________________________ *feeds me.*

3. ______________________________
______________________________ *feeds me.*

4. ______________________________
______________________________ *feeds me.*

5. ______________________________
______________________________ *feeds me.*

6. ______________________________
______________________________ *feeds me.*

7. ____
________________________________ *feeds me.*

8. ____
________________________________ *feeds me.*

9. ____
________________________________ *feeds me.*

When we feel "fed" or have a sense of fullness, we are experiencing healing. That is medicine.

B. When in your life have you felt most fully alive? Where were you? What were you doing? Was anyone else around? How did your body feel? Your mind? Your spirit? Take some time to recall and write down, or draw, whatever images, sounds, or feelings are rising in you right now. Revel in it!

- ____
- ____
- ____
- ____
- ____

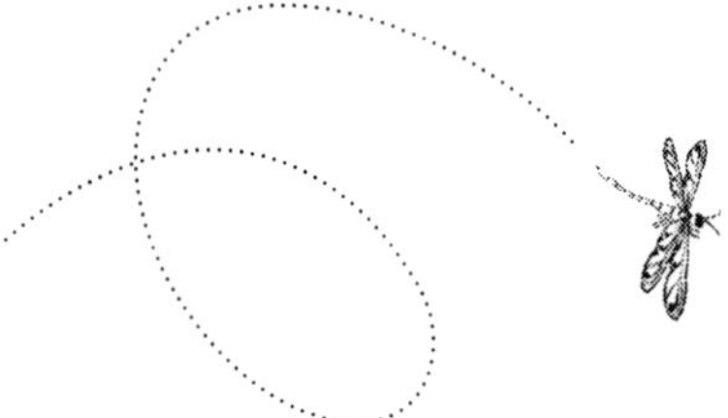

Practice

Writing Your Own Prescription Slips

When we are not feeling well physically, it is common practice to go the doctor. She does her examination, and depending on what she finds, often whips out her prescription pad. We then go to the pharmacist who fills a bottle with pills and places a sticker with instructions on how to take the medication. We trust that if we follow the directions we will see an improvement in our condition.

But where do you go when your heart, spirit, and soul are not feeling so great?

Practice

Prescribing for the Soul

This practice involves you consulting your inner spiritual physician. Start with how you want to feel: joyful, calm, balanced, energized, content, happy, fulfilled, useful?

- *I would like to feel* ______________________________
  ____.

Next take a few moments to connect with your heart (where your inner spiritual physician's office is located) and ask her to prescribe some activities to help bring you closer to how you want to feel.

Now it's time for you to get your pen or crayon, whip out your prescription pad, and write. Trust what comes from your heart, however simple or silly it may seem to your mind. Empower yourself!

Create your own prescription slip, signed with your very own illegible signature, to make it real.

Examples:

- Walk in nature three times a week.
- Watch a funny movie once a week.
- Buy flowers for kitchen countertop and smell them three times a day.
- Turn off anything that beeps by 8:00 p.m.
- Set up an altar.
- Pray every morning and night.
- Volunteer once a week.
- Cook.
- Bring yourself out on a date.
- Make play dates with friends.
- Soak in a bubble bath with candles three times a week.

Write as many prescription slips as you need: daily, weekly, monthly. Now take your own prescriptive medicine regularly and see how you feel in one week, one month, one year. Like any practice, you have to *do* it for it to work. Trust your intuition. Practice taking your own medicine and notice if your symptoms persist. If they do, you may have to go deeper. Patience and practice will pay off.

Original Medicine

Traditional Native American wisdom takes the concept of medicine a step further, believing that we all come to Earth with our own unique gifts to share, called our *original medicine*. That means that you have a special destiny here. You have a unique purpose on this planet, specific to you, no matter what or who you think you are. Your original medicine may look similar to someone else's, but it is your unique gift to give. It has your footprint, exclusive to you and to no one else. Spirit knows your gift and is hungry for you to remember it and express your offering in the world.

I believe this, too. Connecting with my medicine was, and continues to be, a crucial part of my own healing.

Practice

Discovering Your Original Medicine

We looked at some of these questions in the "The Practice of Gratitude" chapter. I encourage you to answer them from where you are now and notice if any of your responses have changed. Please be as specific as possible.

- Who are the people that have most inspired you in the past?
- Who inspires you now?
- Whom do you inspire now? (Dig deep and don't be shy—you are greater than you think.)
- Whom would you like to inspire in the future?

Okay, got your answers? Are they different from the answers you gave in the chapter on "The Practice of Gratitude"? These are all clues to uncovering your original medicine.

Experience is not what happens to you. Experience is what you make out of what happens to you.

~ Aldous Huxley

Medicine Circle

Not sure what your medicine is yet? Thinking perhaps that you are the one exception who came into the world with no original medicine? Feeling a little lost?

Not to worry—as unique as you are, you are not *that* special that you have no gift. Truth be told, you probably have many gifts that have been covered over by years of self-doubt, conditioning, and judgment (conscious or unconscious) from your original family, friends, and culture.

Our culture steals our visions and tells us to grow up, be responsible, realistic, and stop being so childish. As a result, we have suffered tremendously as we no longer engage in initiatory rites of passage from childhood to adulthood. Long gone are the days when it was customary for elders of the tribe to bring the youngsters out into the wild for four days and four nights, without food or water, to commune with nature, sit in a circle made of stones—a medicine circle—and pray for a vision that their life purpose may be revealed.

Often these youngsters would communicate fears of being alone in the forest at night. David Wagoner's poem "Lost" beautifully illustrates and assures us that if we are willing to stand still, turn down the volume of real or imagined ghosts and doubts that so often haunt us, the unknown may reveal a "powerful stranger." That stranger is the one that looks back at you in the mirror every morning, pleading with you to find your power and medicine. We get closer to doing this by situating ourselves in the present moment.

The good news is that you don't have to go out into the forest with no food or water for four days and nights to connect with your life purpose. (Of course, you can if you are so inclined—under the apprenticeship of an experienced vision quest guide, please.) Here, we are going to suggest a simple yet powerful practice that you can do in your own backyard.

Practice

Making Your Own Medicine Circle

Throughout time, ancient cultures around the world have created sacred stone circles to use in prayer and ceremony, with the intention of bringing them closer to Spirit. Typically, the stones are anchored in the four cardinal directions (north, south, east, and west.) You can make your own medicine circle, either symbolically (you may want to use the Sacred Space Altar you created earlier) or physically.

The power the circle holds is created by your own intention.

Find a place in nature; your backyard or nearby park is fine, unless you choose to adventure farther afield. Choose four rocks and place them in a circle large enough for you to sit inside. (You can also do this indoors if you don't have access to a place outside; just *imagine* it is someplace in nature.) Each rock will represent one of the four cardinal directions. Find out which direction is which if you don't know. (Google maps can help with this!)

Each direction holds a different energy, with different attributes, to help you in harmonizing your own energies and attributes. At different times you may find you are drawn to different directions. No direction is better than another; all are equal in their power and gifts. The attributes given to each direction can vary from tribe to tribe and region to region. This is what I have used over the years:

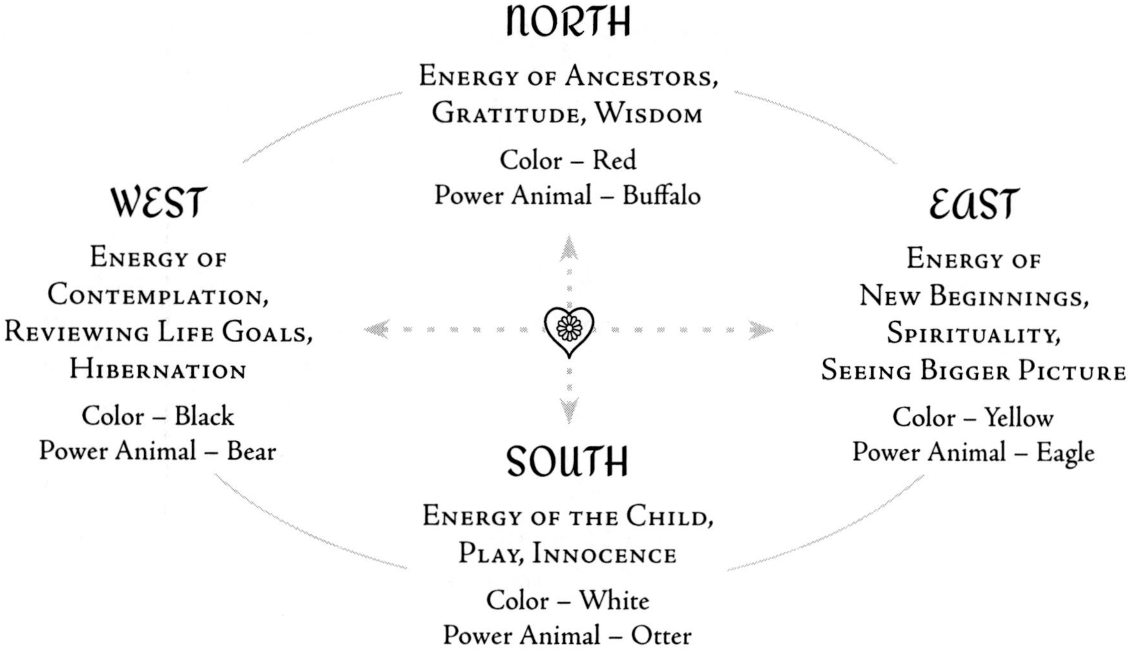

NORTH

Energy of Ancestors, Gratitude, Wisdom

Color – Red
Power Animal – Buffalo

WEST

Energy of Contemplation, Reviewing Life Goals, Hibernation

Color – Black
Power Animal – Bear

EAST

Energy of New Beginnings, Spirituality, Seeing Bigger Picture

Color – Yellow
Power Animal – Eagle

SOUTH

Energy of the Child, Play, Innocence

Color – White
Power Animal – Otter

I also honor the directions of Father Sky (above), Mother Earth (below), and the Heart (center).

Once you have chosen your location and set your rocks in place, spend some time in reflection outside of the circle and ask that this circle may be a place of mystery and power for you to connect more fully with your own energy and attributes, some of which may not be known to you at this moment. Stay outside the circle as long as you need to, and when you are ready, ask permission from the Great Mystery (whatever that means to you) to enter the circle.

Once inside the circle, notice if there are any particular directions you are drawn to. You may want to take some time to sit facing each direction before choosing your position; it's up to you. Play with it and take time to explore within the circle. Take as much time as you need, giving yourself permission just to sit and dream and ask for guidance in revealing clues to your original medicine. Notice everything that comes: colors, symbols, memories, feelings. Remember that once you are holding a high intention, there is no way you can do this incorrectly; just do what feels right for you. It may feel strange at first—it probably will—but don't let that put you off. Discoveries are found in unfamiliar territory.

If you set up your Medicine Circle in a public place, it's a good idea to dismantle it so no one else can enter your sacred place—charged with your intentions and sacred prayers—without your permission. If it is in a place exclusive to you, you may want to leave it intact so you can visit time and time again. Your medicine circle can be a place where you go with the specific intention of asking for help in connecting with your original medicine (or anything that is on your mind). Remember to hold the questions lightly, with an air of wonder and curiosity, rather than demanding an answer. Allow for surprises, new questions, and dreams to emerge. That will help clear the way for the unknown to enter.

I suggest writing down anything that is revealed to you while inside the circle, even and especially if it doesn't make sense to you.

If this practice does not appeal to you for any reason, no worries. You know how to create sacred space from our earlier chapter or just lie down with some relaxing music of your choice and ask the same questions.

Medicine Shield

Traditionally, members of different Native American tribes made (and still make) their own medicine shields. These shields serve as a spiritual protection, as opposed to a physical protection in battle. The shield is the personal flag of its maker. The prolific writer, M. Scott Momaday, describes the plains-warrior relationship with his shield as, "My shield stands for me, and I stand for my shield. I am and I am my shield!" He goes on to say, "The shield is involved in the story. The shield is its own story. When the shield is made visible it means: Here is the story. Enter into it and be created. The story tells of your real being."

The medicine shield can be compared to a coat of arms, a family crest or emblem associated with a particular surname, region, or team, which depicts colors, symbols, and attributes representing the name.

However, the medicine shield differs in that it is exclusive to the bearer. No two shields are the same. Your shield reflects your original medicine. It is a mirror for your soul. Your greatest protection and power in life is to know yourself.

I encourage you to research your own roots for the medicine practices of your ancestors. Irish? Hispanic? Asian? French? African? Middle Eastern? All cultures have rich traditions to draw upon. Calling in and connecting with your own ancestors can be a powerful practice in unveiling your personal medicine.

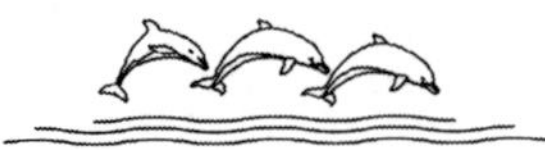

Practice

Making Your Medicine Shield

Shields were traditionally made with rawhide stretched over a hoop, but you can use a poster-sized piece of watercolor paper, a piece of canvas, or plain fabric stretched around an embroidery circle, or opt for a 14-inch circular cake sheet. Be as simple or elaborate as you like. All you need to do is start with a large circle.

Allow images to appear by gently asking yourself these questions:

- *What are my gifts, strengths, vulnerabilities?*
- *What has been revealed to me in the medicine circle?*
- *What is my original medicine?*

As mentioned earlier, it's not about demanding a clear answer. It's more about getting curious about the questions and seeing what feelings, images, or impulses rise up to meet you. You can decorate your shield with symbols, colors, power animals, or anything else that feels right to you. Try and stay away from words if you can, to avoid the temptation to create it from your head. Use any combination of mediums you like: collage, crayons, paint, glitter, feathers, objects from nature, or whatever you are drawn to.

You cannot do this the wrong way. Letting go of a need or expectation for it to look a certain way can free you up to create a new story from right now, in the present, one that inspires you to live into your truest nature, embracing all your strengths and vulnerabilities, living each day to the fullest, as if it were your last.

Once you have made your shield, take a step away from it. Be curious about its maker. What does the shield say about this person? What is not being said but is suggested by the piece? Sit with your shield for a time and write a sentence or an affirmation that best describes the bearer of the shield.

For example, you can start it like this:

- *My authentic self is* ______________________________
  ____.

Go on—be bold, daring, fabulous, kind, fierce, compassionate, funny, caring, loving, adventurous, limitless! There is no one in the world exactly like you.

Kathy's Story

My journey began with a shattered soul, a dark spirit, and a wounded heart. That is what a total mental breakdown felt like to me. That was nine months ago. I was running a highly stressful but successful business that lacked in the rewards that I so desperately needed, such as fulfillment and happiness. When I was not working, I was numbing my mind with self-loathing, drugs, alcohol, and a destructive relationship. Everything was spiraling out of control, as if I were on a runaway train and nobody was left on it but me. I felt so alone, and I hated the only person left on board. I was suicidal and felt like there were no options left. I had no clue how to quit abusing substances, and at that point it was the only thing that gave me some sort of relief. My two friends created an intervention for me, and two days later I was in New Mexico.

My therapist suggested I take a workshop with Pasha. I honestly did not want to do it, as I felt I had absolutely no artistic ability, but what did I really have to lose? So I signed up and attended. I ended up loving it and going every week!

Each class gave me new insights into my very essence that I had never known about myself. Through different projects we were assigned to do, I discovered I did have a creative and artistic side. One of my favorites was making my medicine shield. Before we made it, we walked a labyrinth. When entering, I tried my best to clear my mind so I could receive whatever divine message the Great

Spirit would bless me with that day. When I got to the middle, I opened my arms and hands and just breathed, knowing something special was happening even if it was not clear at that moment. When I came out, I lifted my arms, head, and soul to the sun, thanking it for its light and warmth. I remember specifically feeling the warmth on my face and remembering the innocence and peace that I felt when I was a child playing in the woods. It was truly amazing to just be present with nature and all her divine beauty!

After the walk we were invited to make our own shields, to reflect our true self. I ended up loving my piece. I told Pasha, "I can't believe this came out of me!" Pasha said, "Just think of all the other unknown gifts you have. What else is waiting and wanting to make itself known to you?" Wow, thinking in that way has opened up doors for my soul to play in places I would not allow it to go before.

Here I am, nine months later, sober and content with my life, for the most part. I have my medicine shield as the focal point in my living room, as a reminder that it's okay to feel lost or scared sometimes. Even when I feel like a failure and I'm trying my hardest to be a better person, I can look at the painting and know I'm not failing. My path has simply taken me to a new and unexpected route. I know in my heart that with hard work and compassion toward myself I will reach that place in the middle where the sun will be shining on my face again!

Walking the Beauty Way

In the chapter on "The Practice of Gratitude," I mentioned how labyrinths are symbols of our unique journey. Actually walking a labyrinth will be explored more in the next chapter. For now, contemplate walking as a way of discovering your original medicine. Simply by walking with intention you can move toward your life purpose.

Read the following prayer, from the Navajo tradition. It beautifully expresses what it means to open to all the beauty in ourselves and our lives. Softening our breath, our gaze, and our hearts allows us to have a greater openness to life, allowing more beauty to readily shine forth. The beauty is always there, waiting for you to stop and notice its quiet presence.

The Beauty Way

In Beauty may I walk.

All day long may I walk.

Through the returning seasons may I walk.

Beautifully will I possess again.

Beautifully birds . . .

Beautifully joyously birds . . .

On the trail marked with pollen may I walk.

With grasshoppers about my feet may I walk.

With deer about my feet may I walk.

With Beauty may I walk.

With Beauty before me may I walk.

With Beauty behind me may I walk.

With Beauty above me may I walk.

In old age, wandering on a trail of Beauty,
lively may I walk.

In old age, wandering on a trail of Beauty,
living again may I walk.

It is finished in Beauty.

It is finished in Beauty.

Conclude this prayer with your own affirmation. For example:

- *My authentic self is powerful, beautiful, loving, and unafraid. My original medicine is* ______________ ______________________________________ ______________________________________.

9

The Practice of True Nature

Climb the mountain and get their good tidings. Nature's peace will flow into you, while cares will fall off like autumn leaves.

~ John Muir

The word *nature* comes from the Latin word *natura*, which means "to be born." Everything born has an essence. *You* have an essence—it is unique to you—so does each blade of grass, cocker spaniel, racehorse, cat, sparrow. We equate the *essence* of a thing to its innate nature. If it is alive, it has an essence!

In the Celtic tradition (similar to most indigenous cultures), the Earth is revered as a wildly alive and vibrant being. Every aspect of nature interacts in a mysterious and harmonious way, even if it does not appear that way to the human eye. I recall my grandparents, who were farmers, calling the fields by different names. When you think about it, mountains, rivers, parks, streets, and highways all have names. From a human perspective, when we give something a name we begin to develop a relationship with it.

The name *Ireland* is derived from the ancient Irish word *Eriu*, which in Irish mythology was the name of a daughter of the Tuatha De Dannan. She is known as the matron goddess of the land. The wise ones who named this luscious, verdant, wild, windy, and wet island knew things that have long been lost to us. Thankfully, they are reemerging into our collective consciousness as more and more of us yearn to live more harmoniously, joyfully, and authentically. With reference to the great Hopi poem, "We are the ones we have been waiting for."

Conscious femininity is an awareness of the energy of the rock and the love in the bird, the tree, the sunset. An awareness of the harmony of all things, of living in the world soul. You feel the harmony of the whole Universe, in the marrow of your bones.

~ Marion Woodman, *The Conscious Feminine*

Now it is time to discover and reconnect with the light and beauty of your essence, your true nature, so you can shine out into the world and make it a better place—not only for yourself but for everyone.

Practice

Affirming Your Connection to Nature

Try practicing the following affirmation for one full day. Repeat it at transitions times, like when you leave the house, when you begin a new project or task, before a meal, etc.

> Today, I will see myself as an extension of all that is natural and beautiful in the world.

We are constantly being reminded how out of balance Mother Earth is, due to a myriad of factors. (I hope these reminders will call each of us to act.) Unfortunately, overwhelm can set in. We can feel overcome with grief and uncertainty and turn the other way. It is at times like these that we most likely turn away from what is natural and beautiful in the world, and also in ourselves. What we need to do is turn toward what is beautiful, internally and externally.

In difficult times you should always carry something beautiful in your mind.

~ Blaise Pascal

Nature is a magical mirror that is constantly reflecting back to us all that we need to know. It's time to look with wide eyes and an open heart.

Practice

Relating to Nature

Take a minute or two and choose five things from the natural world or animal kingdom to describe yourself. Then write down the aspects that relate to you.

Examples:

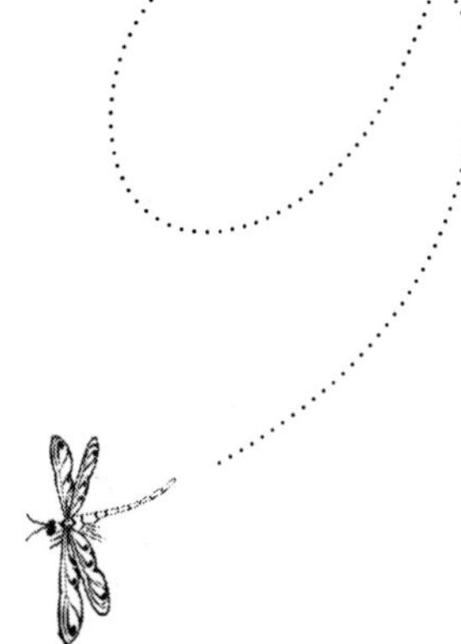

- A dragonfly is like me because it is fairylike, magical, mysterious.
- A lotus flower is like me because its roots are in the mud and it grows out of murky waters.
- A sunflower is like me because I'm always reaching for the sun.
- A horse is like me because I'm sensitive, empathetic, and love community.
- A lioness is like me because I'm protective and fierce.

Now you try it:

1. A ______________________________________
   ___________ is like me because _____________
   ____.

2. A ______________________________
__________ is like me because __________
______________________________.

3. A ______________________________
__________ is like me because __________
______________________________.

4. A ______________________________
__________ is like me because __________
______________________________.

5. A ______________________________
__________ is like me because __________
______________________________.

Spring is here and nobody knows how it happened.

~ ANTONIO MACHADO

Compare and Despair

Nature follows a rhythm and cycle that goes beyond the mind. It is hard to imagine that a barren-looking tree in February will have buds in March and colorful flowers, fruit, and leaves by summer.

When an aspen loses it leaves in October, does it feel depressed? Does it feel inferior to the mighty oak across the way? Could the redwing blackbird think the duck's call is cooler than hers? Does the lilac think it's ugly if the butterfly sails past and lands on the daisy nearby?

I don't know for sure, but I doubt it.

Humans are the ones who do this, all the time: compare, judge, and have opinions about what and who is better, more successful, thinner, richer, and more beautiful. Why do we do this?

Because we don't know who we are.

I have heard the great Indian saint and spiritual teacher Mata Amritanandamayi (Amma) give us the analogy of the ocean to illustrate this point. The ignorant wave says, "Hey, look at me! I am bigger and mightier than that wave." Another day it might say, "Oh, I am such a tiny and weak wave. All those other waves are so much more powerful." But the wise wave consistently knows and says, "I am water."

Comparison is what keeps you separate from seeing who you truly are. It serves no purpose other than damaging and betraying your soul.

So go ahead and give full expression to whatever type of a wave you are in any given moment. Just know you are water, and let your inner wave loose!

Today you are you!
That is truer than true!
There is no one alive
who is you-er than you!

~ Dr. Seuss

Practice

Ending Comparisons

The next time you notice yourself comparing yourself to anyone or anything, try asking yourself this question instead:

Who am I?

Resist the impulse to answer it. Just ask, and keep asking it over and over again, without demanding an answer. Each time you ask the question, infuse it with as much warmth and wonder as you can.

You can also ask:

Who is comparing?

Over time, see what happens. You may just discover how magnificent it is to be water.

Being in Nature

In difficult and turbulent times we should endeavor to stay close to one simple thing in nature.

~ RAINER MARIA RILKE

How often do you spend time in nature? I don't mean your power walk, charging across the park. I mean just chillin', kicking back, listening to and observing the landscape of which you are a part. Breathing in and out. No agenda. Nothing to accomplish or figure out. Just being.

Too busy? No time? You, and the planet, are worth making the effort and finding the time. Nature needs you to spend time in Her, as much as we need Her to breathe and eat. It's a reciprocal relationship.

Whoever you are, and wherever you live, take the time to find one special place in nature. You can go to this place whenever you need to unburden your heart and your mind. Simply sit and breathe, or tell the natural world your worries and concerns. Nature has a mysterious and magical way of lifting the burden, so you don't feel so alone in your confusion.

Rainer Maria Rilke, the Bohemian-Austrian poet of the early 1900s, writes beautifully about this in his "Ninth Duino Elegy." He beseeches us to **"praise this world to the angel."** He invites us to imagine that this angel is blind and cannot see all the natural wonders that surround us every day—the ones we so often take for granted.

Could you describe a sunset? Have you ever tried? What does it look like when a raindrop hits a pink, almost opened, rose petal? How does grass move when a gust of wind passes by? What path does a gold aspen leaf take on its flight from the branch to the ground? Could you describe the shapes of clouds and how they change in the blink of an eye? What does freshly cut grass smell like? What is the difference between walking on sand or gravel? How do you know which birds are singing and which ones are crying? How does it feel to stand in the middle of a cold stream of water? On the top of a mountain? On the bank of a river? At the edge of a cliff? To sit in the middle of a cornfield? To watch a colony of ants, busy at work? Look up to the top of a redwood? What are the sounds you hear in the forest? How many stars can you count? How is the sky different at night? Where is the moon? How does it change its shape? How does it shine differently than the sun?

Make up some questions of your own. Use your imagination and have fun!

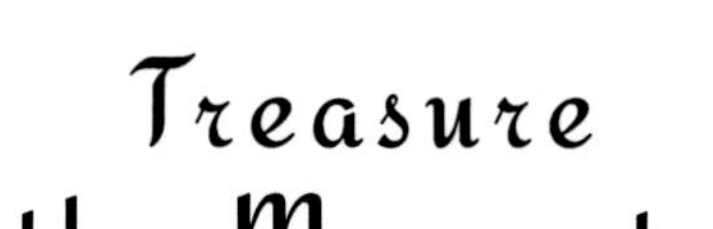

Treasure the Moments

Notes-to-a-Blind-Angel

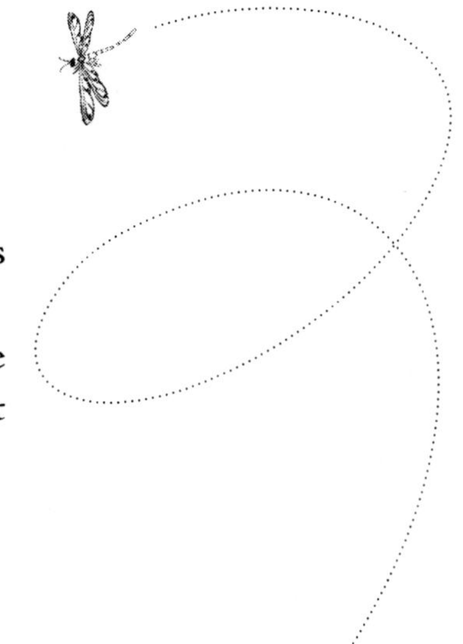

What if you were to become the eyes, ears, and nose of this blind angel?

How would you share and describe your experience of walking in the world? Try it for one day, and notice if it changes your experience of being in the world.

You may just find yourself wanting to do it every day.

Practice

Moving in Nature Meditation

If you can move and breathe, you can practice this. It doesn't require any special powers, and you don't have to look "spiritual" while you are doing it. No one else has to know. All you have to do is open your door and move through space. If you can find a nearby park, quiet road, beach, mountain, or woods great. If not, just circle the block a few times.

When we allow ourselves to connect with our natural surroundings, nature has a mysterious and magical way of helping us to slow down our breathing, thereby slowing down our thoughts. She lures us deep inside, where a stillness and peace are patiently and passionately waiting for us to return. If you can't do it nature, do it on your way to the train or bus station. Do it while looking out a window. Nature is everywhere.

These steps of the meditation practice will help you more fully engage with nature:

> Bring your attention to the top of your head. Look up at the sky. Imagine all your thoughts being released into the vastness. The sky is endless, big enough to carry all your thoughts away for the time you are practicing this. Breathe in a new breath, full of white light, from the top of your head all the way down to your feet.

1. Bring your attention to your feet. Feel the solid ground beneath you, supporting you, holding you close to the heart of the Earth. The depth of this loving support is limitless. Let go of any debris that may not have been fully released from step one. Breathe in a new breath full of red, vibrant, grounding energy from your feet all the way up to the top of your head.

2. Bring your attention to your heart. Close your eyes. Feel your heart softening with each inhale and expanding on every exhale. Imagine you are breathing into your heart from all directions: front, back, and sides. At the same time, breathe in a white-filled breath from the top of your head and a red-filled breath from the soles of your feet. Let the breaths and colors meet and merge in your heart. Breathe in this pink color and let it completely fill your heart with **love.**

3. Open your eyes and look around at all the love, however it may be revealed. Imagine that everything and everyone you see is loving you and longing to be loved by you. Breathe in unconditional love, breathe out unconditional love.

4. With this same awareness, take a step. Step into love. Take another one. Start walking with this new awareness, conscious of every breath, every step. Focus your attention on your breath and your step. Become acutely, and softly, aware of each foot as it meets the ground, each breath as it enters your nose and expands your heart. When your foot touches the Earth, imagine she is whispering, "I love you."

5. When thoughts begin to intrude (which they will), just bring the focus back to the sensation of your breath and your step.

6. When you start thinking again and again and again—no need to fret or judge—just calmly and steadily ask: *Who is thinking?*

7. You can do this for a while, then try responding with *I am. I am thinking.* Then ask: *Who is this I?*

8. No need to answer—just walk.

Practice this for five minutes at a time, as often as you can, slowly building up the length of time. Over time, watch as all the labels, identities, and stories of your little "I" fall away: *love is all that remains.* Love is your true nature, but you have to discover that for yourself.

This is a practice you can use for the rest of your life.

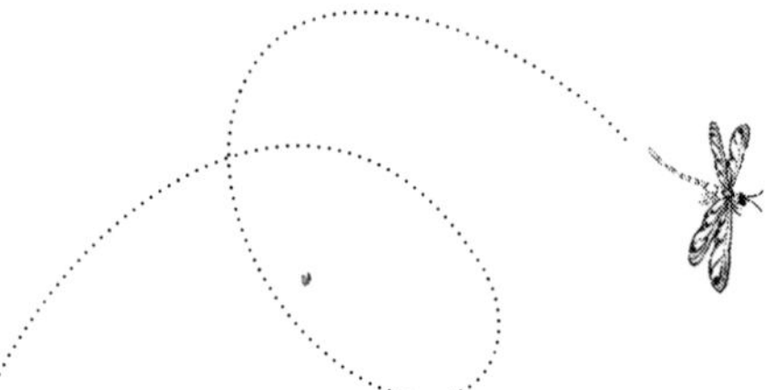

Practice

Wonder Walking

Another walking practice you can incorporate is a wonder walk. No prep, just take your young and innocent self with you and walk—anywhere—simply walk. Pretend nothing has a name yet, nothing has an association with it. Your eyes are wide open and curious. Observe everything you can see, smell, and touch with a detached bewilderment.

Change your route often!

While I was out on a wonder walk one day near my house, in an area cared for by the Nature Conservancy, I noticed a sign I had passed by at least ninety-nine times. I stopped to read it for the first time.

> *When conditions are right, nature can reclaim an area quickly.*
>
> *After the reservoir was removed, a shallow pond remained in its place, fed by slow flow from groundwater, springs, and upstream reservoirs. It didn't take long for native cattails, redwing blackbirds, and ducks to find their way to this new, life-supporting habitat.*
>
> *Although nature always reclaims its own, it can make a speedier recovery with a little help. The Nature Conservancy removes non-native plants . . . so that our native shrubs, trees, and flowers—and the creatures that depend on them—can thrive.*

It was one of those "AH-HA" moments. The light bulb in my heart-mind burned bright!

What is true for nature is true for us.

Playtime!

What Are the Right Conditions for Your True Nature to Thrive?

Loosen up and play with this. You may want to get a big piece of paper to collage, draw, or write. Keep it someplace handy, so you can keep adding to it.

Carry the following question around with you and allow the answers to emerge naturally. Don't force it, but do bring your attention to it as if your life depended on it. It does!

> What "non-native" plants (in the form of thoughts, beliefs, shame, people, places, substances, or anything else that limits you) are overshadowing your environment (lifestyle, place of work, home, body, mind, spirit)?

For example, the inner critic, with its harsh, mean voice that stops us in our tracks, is a weed that chokes innocence and enthusiasm.

- ____

  ____

- ____

  ____

- ______________________________________
  ____

- ______________________________________
  ____

- ______________________________________
  ____

As you discover answers, remember that it is important to distinguish between what serves your past story, and what serves who you are now, and who you are becoming.

Psst! In the same way we can't do anything to "improve" the natural wonders of the world, this is not about improving your nature. You are already a natural wonder of the world, just by being born.

Your nature is perfect in this moment. These practices are offered to help lift the veils that cover up and keep you separate from what is already beautiful and natural about you. So you can experience it, share it, and shine!

The real voyage of discovery consists not in seeking new landscapes but in having new eyes.

~ Marcel Proust

Epic Battles: Burning Boats

Most cultures carry ancient and fantastical stories, dating back hundreds and thousands of years, depicting ferocious battles that ultimately have the potential to save or destroy civilization.

In many such stories the battlefield is symbolic for the warzone of the mind. In order to attain peace and freedom in life, the majority of us fight a long, drawn-out battle between the conflicting parts of ourselves. Sound familiar?

The brilliant scholar and writer John Moriarty, in his book *Invoking Ireland*, shares Ireland's version of this story. It is called the Battle of Magh Tuired.

It goes something like this:

> A long, long time ago, Ireland was inhabited by two very different tribes: the Tuatha de Dannan and the Fomorians. No one is quite sure where the Tuatha de Dannan came from. It is said that when they landed their boats, full of silver and gold, on the shores of Ireland they immediately set them on fire. I imagine they did this so there was no option to turn around and return to where they came from. Moving into unknown territory was the only way forward.
>
> The Tuatha de Dannan loved and respected nature. They bowed down to Her and changed their ways to live at one with Her.
>
> The Fomorians were a different breed altogether. They had no regard for nature and destroyed whatever was in their path to get what they wanted, when they wanted it. After a short time it was clear these two tribes could not share the country and live in peace. War was promptly declared.
>
> It was a long and bloody battle, full of great warriors, as well as great wizards. Magic spells were invoked by both tribes, and each side would go to any lengths to win the fight.
>
> After what seemed like a lifetime, it looked like the Tuatha de Dannan had finally secured a victory. They were overjoyed! Finally, the brutish Fomorians had been put in their place. Lavish festivities broke out throughout their camp. The sounds of clinking goblets,

wild fiddle music, dancing, and loud bagpipes filled the air. What the Tuatha did not know was that while they were celebrating, the chief Fomorian wizard made himself invisible. Unnoticed, he walked straight into the heart of the celebrations and stole the Tuatha's great harp, named *Harmonizes Us to All Things*.

When the last goblet was raised, the last jig danced, and the last tune sung, all the Tuatha fell into a deep sleep, not knowing that their beloved harp had been stolen.

The next day a heavy cloud set over the camp. There was not a joyful sound to be heard. Not even the larks or wrens could muster up a tune. As the day went on, all one could hear were the grumblings of a restless and disgruntled tribe, who now sounded like Fomorians! No one knew what was wrong, until the chief poet discovered that the harp was stolen. With the theft of *Harmonizes Us to All Things*, the song of Ireland was gone, too.

The chief poet noticed that only one man had not succumbed to the ignorant Fomorian ways. His name was Ogma.

When Ogma was questioned as to what it was that made him behave so differently than everyone else. He replied, "There is something greater to me than my life."

What could that be they all wondered? Was it the mountains, the stars?

Ogma said, "Without it, there would be no mountains and no stars. It is only when you surrender your life that you most plentifully derive your life from it."

That is what set Ogma apart. From then on it was the question of Ogma that both bewildered and bothered the songless Tuatha.

Three days after the great harp was stolen, Ogma left and headed straight for the heart of the Fomorian's fortress.

"Telling no one his business, just being the man he was, he walked, no one daring to challenge him, through all outer and inner defenses. Armed doorkeepers making way for him, he entered the fortress at the heart of the country, he took the harp and, as with everyone's permission, he walked back to the shore, taking Ireland's stolen music with him and brought it home to Ireland." (*Invoking Ireland*, p. 28)

The Tuatha were overjoyed and rushed to ask him how he brought home the harp so boldly and gracefully.

He replied: "As we discovered too late, it was by being able to be invisible that Macguarch (the chief Fomorian wizard) stole our music. It was by being able to be visible, all the way out from the ground of my being to their being, that I was able to walk past them, bringing it home. Also, I did not project any obstacles out of myself. I didn't project those monsters and dragons that so often contest the hero's way. There is no part of my mind that I am not at ease with, that isn't at ease with me." (*Invoking Ireland*, p. 29)

With the return of the harp, harmony was restored to the land once again. Blackbirds sang, poems were recited, jigs danced, and lovers loved. Finally, the Fomorians and the Tuatha we united by a common question, posed by Ogma.

I believe that the question of Ogma is: *who am I?*

That is the hidden question that runs through every fairy tale, myth, and story ever told. It runs through life itself. The epic and endless battle going on in your own mind—and whether the battle is won or lost—hinges on this question.

You are here to discover the answer for yourself.

This tale shows us that when we really know ourselves, nothing is impossible. Your greatest strength and defense is knowing yourself.

Practice

Recapturing the Harp

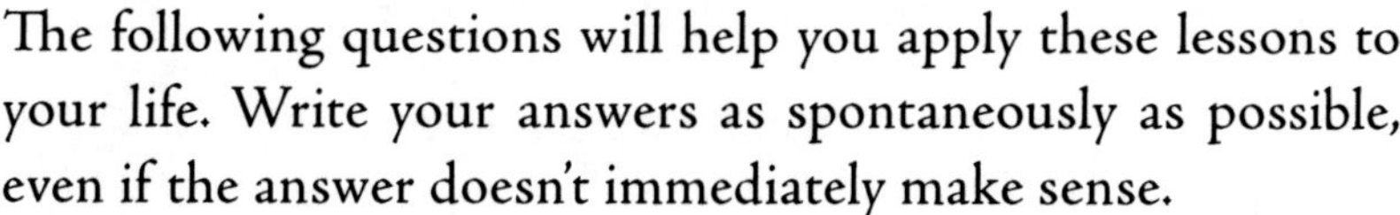

The following questions will help you apply these lessons to your life. Write your answers as spontaneously as possible, even if the answer doesn't immediately make sense.

- Name three battlegrounds of your life.
- What battles are you willing to let go, or at least declare a truce?
- Are you willing to surrender the small version you have of yourself for the rest of this journey?

Recognizing when your Fomorian mind is acting up can be helpful.

- What does "winning" look like to your Fomorian mind?

- Do you know what your triggers are?
- How do you continue to feed your Fomorian mind?

Give yourself permission not to know the answers, to loosen up and play with the questions. Accept your own thoughts and feelings as they arise.

The Tuatha de Dannan intuitively knew that if they had a way back they may not have readily accessed the courage required of them to keep going.

- What boats (thoughts, stories, habits, beliefs) do you need to burn in order to move forward?
- How does attachment to your "boats" limit your ability to make discoveries?
- What does the harp symbolize for you?
- What are the ways you fight against your own true nature?
- What are the things/people/situations that Harmonize You to All Things?
- What has been stolen from you while you were sleeping (unconscious)?
- What do you need to retrieve?
- What are the monsters and dragons (negative self talk) you project onto your path?
- How can you be more visible?
- What song do you want to sing?

- What are all the ways you can bring your song to the world?

If you have a favorite myth or story, apply similar questions, knowing that it is the nature of everlasting stories to reflect back to us our true nature.

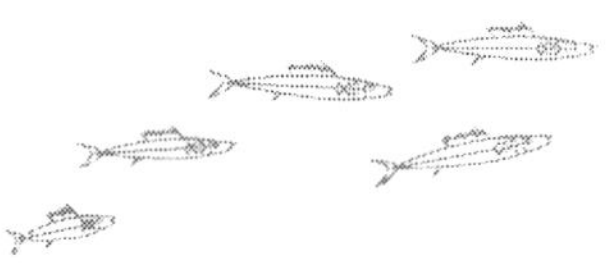

10

The Practice of Releasing

You have everything you need. This is not a practice of picking up new theories and concepts. It is a practice of letting go of the thoughts, stories, and behaviors that no longer serve you.

We shall not cease from exploration. And the end of all our exploring will be to arrive where we started and know the place for the first time.

~ T. S. ELIOT

Your Mythic Journey

Who am I?

Why am I here?

These questions have been asked since the dawn of humankind. And they have been answered, consistently, throughout the ages through stories. We looked briefly at myths in "The Practice of Beginning" chapter and again in the previous chapter. Now we will plumb the depths.

Joseph Campbell, the late and brilliant mythologist and writer, is the master of extracting and highlighting how important ancient myths are in helping us navigate the challenges of contemporary living. He helps us see how connected we are as a human race. It doesn't seem to matter where the story is set, who it is about, or how many thousands or hundreds of years ago it took place. There are qualities and questions to this life journey that **affect us all.** Through myths, we can identify with a more universal story, one that can help free us to make fresh choices and imagine more brightly and dream bigger and access the courage already inside us, so that we can venture into unknown territory.

Let's have a look at four main aspects of any seeker's journey, as identified by Campbell.

1. **The Call**

    It usually comes unannounced and can look like anything. You're doing the dishes and suddenly realize you can't bear to give one more slide presentation. It's over. You have no experience in any other area, but you know you can't go back. Or your relationship disintegrates, with a text message, just when you're about to move in together. Or on a routine trip to the doctor, during lunch, you learn you have cancer.

    Whatever it is, wherever you are, it's generally unwelcome and inconvenient.

    You don't know it yet, but this is your big chance, your lucky break, your call to adventure and discovery. Initially, it can suck. It's scary and uncomfortable and fills you with fear. You want to pretend it's not real and it doesn't matter. Maybe you can. Mostly you can't.

    Suddenly, out of the blue, you realize you are living half of a life.

    Don't go back to sleep.

Practice

Listening for the Call

Remember those calls out of your comfort zone? We've talked about your comfort zone throughout this workbook. Practices from the first two chapters explored these in detail. Review those practices now.

- Has your comfort zone shifted?
- Feeling any new ones brewing on the horizon?
- Can you identify any calls you ignored along the way?

2. **The Separation**

After the call comes responding to the call. You have to leave your comfort zone to discover the unknown half. There is no way around it. You don't have to leave fearlessly, you can step out shaking in your shoes, bringing the fears and doubts along. Just be willing to walk out the door.

This is a threshold where the practice of releasing is key. **What behaviors do you need to let go of in order to take this next step?**

Death is not the greatest loss in life. The greatest loss is what dies inside us while we live.

~ Norman Cousins

- Caretaker?
- Provider?

- Smart one?
- Rock of Gibraltar?
- Control freak?
- Professional?
- People pleaser?

Please add your own here:

- ______________________________
  ____
- ______________________________
  ____
- ______________________________
  ____
- ______________________________
  ____
- ______________________________
  ____

In addition to roles, this stage could involve actions—anything from leaving a job, turning off your television, cutting up your credit cards, facing any type of an addiction (food, substances, gambling, love, sex), addressing an abusive past or present, leaving a loveless relationship, donating clothes to your local consignment store, or moving away from home.

It doesn't matter how big or small the first step is. What matters is that you take an action.

You are separating from what is comfortable to you on one level, yet it keeps you stuck feeling like you are living half a life.

This part can feel lonely. It is important to remember that you are leaving behind behaviors that you identify with, not leaving behind who you are. Who you are is unchanging, and you are not alone, though it may feel like you are.

- Remember: you have practices to help you take another breath, another step.
- Remember: reach out and ask for support if you need to; there is no shame in asking for help. You don't know who you may be helping by doing so.
- Remember: look inward for support, too. Try this:

Breathe in: *I*
Breathe out: *AM*
and in the gap between the
next inhale: *ENOUGH*

Any of the earlier breathing practices in this book will also be useful here.

We need to be willing to give up the life we planned in order to live the life that is waiting for us.

~ JOSEPH CAMPBELL

3. The Initiation

In myths, impossible tasks are usually presented to the seeker during this stage. Trials and tribulations will appear out of left field. Any doubt you ever had about not being good enough will surface. It's okay. Let them come to the surface, challenge them, rest, and then keep going. Take it as a sign that you are on your way into unchartered territory—and discovery.

Epic stories illustrate this stage by sorting the wheat from the chaff, descending to the underworld, walking through fire, going without food or water for days at a time.

No one knows how long the initiation stage will last. Myths remind us it could take three days, three months, three years, or three hundred years.

Three is sacred and common in mythology, most likely related to the cycle of birth, death, and rebirth. In this cycle, a part of us does die. It is the part that no longer serves your new vision.

Renaming what you think of as a "bad patch" in your journey can help give you the strength to keep going. Naming your trials and tribulations as initiations can help you emerge from them victoriously as opposed to seeing yourself as a victim.

Practice

Transitioning from Victim to Thriver

- Name the initiations you have gone through in the past.
- What have you discovered about yourself as a result of going through this?

- What are you currently going through?

4. The Return

This is the stage where we start to integrate our experiences, infused with the wisdom we have earned. We return to the world altered and changed, and we share our stories.

Do not be surprised if people close to you do not want to hear about your discoveries. Your growth may feel threatening to them for a multitude of reasons that have nothing to do with you. In Louise Hay's popular book, *You Can Heal Your Life*, she suggests going about your own healing and leaving everyone else alone. Not everyone wants to hear all about how your fantastic insights can help on their journey. They may be just fine in their comfortable chair and not be interested in getting off of it. They might be unaware of their fears. This path is not for everyone.

But I say: tell your story, sing your song. It is not up to you if the people you want to hear it, don't, or won't. Release the expectation of getting a reaction, and let the sharing be your affirmation. And who knows? You may inspire an important stranger to embark upon a journey into an unknown landscape and never even know it.

It is your responsibility to return to life changed and altered by your direct experiences. On the surface, it may look like nothing has happened, but your soul knows. The reward shows up in how you live your life. You have a deeper sense of what you are made of and who you are. Life will never be the same again.

Heads up: Just when you are comfortable, and it feels like you've got it all figured out, the cycle starts all over again!

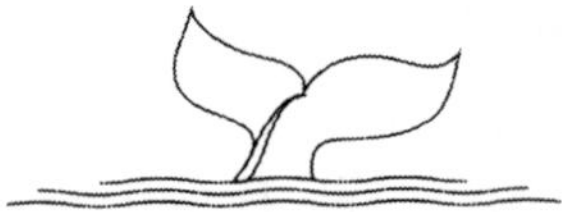

Treasure the Moments

Questions for Reflection

- What part of the Mythic Journey did you most identify with initially?
- And now? Has it changed?
- What aspects of yourself do you need to release, or embrace, in order to move on to the next stage?

You are writing your own myth every day by the thoughts you think and the actions you take.

Your story is not over; it is unfolding.

Practice

Following the Yellow Brick Road

The Wizard of Oz is a great example of a mythic journey, known to many. Dorothy's trek through Oz contains all the elements of a call, separation, initiation, and return.

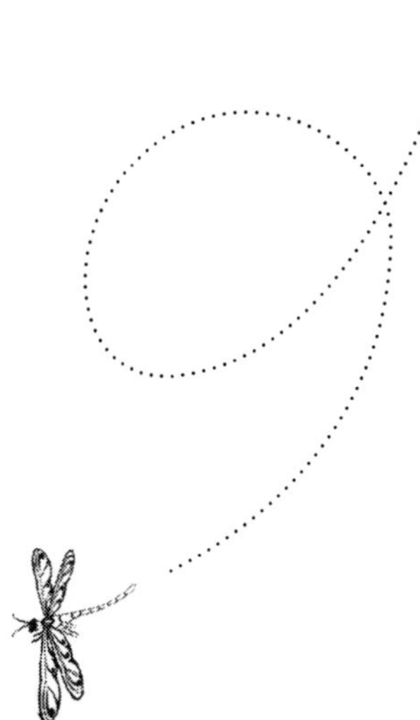

- Which character in the *Wizard of Oz* do you most identify with—and why?
- In your life, have you known wicked witches? Wizards? Flawed companions?
- What do you possess that another has envied? Did you value this?

We each need to find the equivalent in our own lives of the yellow brick road. Are there munchkin voices encouraging you to follow *your* road?

- Where would you like to travel to (real or imagined) that you have never been before?
- What would you like to bring with you?
- What would you like to leave behind?
- How do you want to feel when you get there?

The Three-fold Path of the Labyrinth

Traveler, there is no road; you make the road by walking.

~ ANTONIO MACHADO

Labyrinths have been used by cultures all around the world for thousands of years as a spiritual tool in connecting with one's deepest and highest self. Today they can be found in a wide variety of settings, including churches, businesses, and hospital grounds. Research has shown that walking a labyrinth can help reduce stress and contribute to an overall sense of accomplishment and well-being. Find one in your neighborhood and walk it if you can. It is a wonderful experience!

If you have ever experienced walking a labyrinth, you may have noticed that quite often, when you think you are near the center, a turn comes out of nowhere and you find yourself at the outer edge again. You may feel disappointed, tricked, lost, fed up, and you may want to quit. But suddenly, a sharp left turn brings you deep into the center. It is important to remember that no matter how much the path changes its course, you will always get to the center if you put one foot in front of the next and stay awake.

The labyrinth can be used as a mirror for your life. We don't learn about the labyrinth, we learn about ourselves. Remembering that labyrinths have one way in and one way out, using the three Rs as reference points can be helpful as you walk a labyrinth:

1. **Releasing**

   As you enter the labyrinth you can consciously ask to release anything or anyone that you want to let go. Be as specific as possible. This can be anything from people, ideas, resentments, feelings, shame, guilt, anger, jealousy, self-doubt, etc. You can also release a question, without rushing for or expecting an answer straight away. Notice what thoughts come up and how you feel.

2. **Receiving**

When you reach the center, stop. Imagine you are at the center of your very being. Spend as much time as you need to here. Breathe deeply and fully. Connect with the fullness of the present moment. Maybe you receive an answer, a feeling, or a question here. Give yourself permission to be surprised by what wants to rise up and be known.

3. **Returning**

This is your time to integrate your experience as you prepare to return to where you started "and know it for the first time." Before you exit the labyrinth, pause and bow to all the known and unknown blessings you have received by making the effort to embark on this silent pilgrimage. How do you want to return and show up for your life?

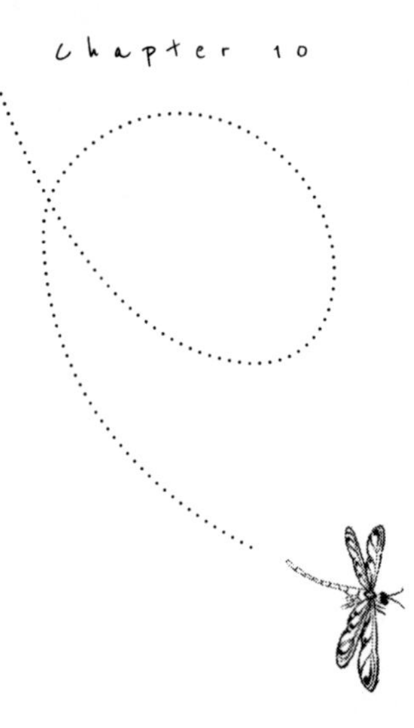

Playtime!

Remembering Your Past to Enlighten Your Future

As with labyrinths, in life we may not know where we are going or what is coming next. But we do know where we have been. The view of where we have been is not a labyrinth but more like a river. As a part of this creative playtime, I invite you to take a deep jump into the river of your life.

You will need a large piece of paper and crayons. We are going to take a swift trip down the River of Consciousness.

You can choose to write and/or illustrate whatever spontaneously comes to your mind, with no censoring. Let your answers flow . . . like a river!

Ready? Go!

- What places did you most like to play in when you were little?
- What did you like to play?
- How would you describe yourself at age five? fourteen? twenty-one?
- Whom did you love?
- When in your life have you felt free? What were you doing?
- What have been the most defining moments of your life so far?

- What have been your greatest joys?
- What have been your deepest sorrows?
- What have been your biggest disappointments?
- What music has been important in your life story?
- What secrets are you hiding?
- Where do you find support?
- Whom do you trust?
- What activities make your spirit soar?
- What do you do to relax?
- What are you ashamed of?
- What are you proud of?
- What were you afraid of as a child?
- What are you afraid of as an adult?
- What secrets did you keep as a kid?
- What was your first job?
- What was your biggest mistake?
- What was your greatest achievement?
- What are the biggest questions you have for your life?
- What are seven words and/or symbols you would use to describe yourself?
- What do you long for?

Okay, put down your crayon, take a breath, and a step back. Be kind.

Stand on the riverbank and have a look at the River of Your Life so far.

- What is not being shown here that you want to include? What is not being said here that needs a voice? Take your time.
- What is being reflected back to you from this river? How do you feel?

Your personal history is not your true identity. You are consciousness itself, the "Light of the World."

~ Eckhart Tolle

However you feel when you look at this, know that it is not *you*. These are only experiences that have shaped your ideas of who you are. This is the half you know.

Release what you *know*, so you can discover who you are.

Map It

Walking the Labyrinth

Okay, we can't walk a labyrinth in a workbook, but you can use the one below to represent your journey through the ten practices of Creative Discovery.

Use this image to make your inner journey visible. Be inspired by the answers to the questions above.

Recall or review your experiences as you explored, created, and discovered the truest *you*. Allow this representation to reflect your answers to *Who am I, Why am I here?*

Mark the challenges and the triumphs along the way.

Apply words, colors, or symbols. No rules—just feel it out.

1. Beginning
2. Not Knowing
3. Gratitude
4. Creating
5. Self-Love
6. Happiness
7. Rest
8. Medicine
9. True Nature
10. Releasing

Congratulations for giving yourself permission to not know, play, and practice! That is no small thing—and neither are you. Please feel free to enter and re-enter these practices as often as you like. Share them with your friends and adapt them to best serve you.

Imagine the little kid inside of you is giving you an enthusiastic high five and a hug right now. So am I. It is my hope a few secrets have been revealed to you by now, empowering you to live with more purpose and passion as the one, the *only* YOU.

Message to the Reader

Dear Fellow Discoverers,

The opening of this book and adventure started out with the statement I placed on the back of my business card three years ago:

Dragonfly symbolizes the transcendence
of self-created illusions.
Are you ready?

At that time, I did not realize I still had a few big, self-created illusions of my own to break through! It is clear to me now that this workbook could not have been delivered to you until these illusions were revealed to me and worked though creatively.

During and after each illusion broke down, I found myself returning to the practices in this book—over and over again. Initially, I thought I had lost something. But in a very short time I realized I hadn't lost anything at all. In fact, I gained insight, a fresh perspective, and more space for authenticity, joy, and love to fill my life. Every time I pick up a practice, I am in a different place; seeing this helps and inspires me to keep going deeper.

I share this with you to encourage you to keep participating in this wild ride called your life and I truly hope you find this workbook helpful along the way.

It would be great to meet you in person one day at one of my workshops or retreats! In the meantime please know that you are not alone. There are people just like you, and me, all over the world that are engaged in the work and play of living from the heart and soul. It's not always easy, folks, I know, but it's rewarding and worth it. So please don't ever give up on yourself—the world needs your authenticity and creative spirit, now more than ever!

Oh, and by the way, in case you forgot, you are good enough as you are right now, more beautiful than you know, and more loved than you can even imagine.

Thanks for being a part of my life and letting me be a part of yours.

Bright blessings to you dear one.

With Love,
Pasha

Acknowledgments

So many generous hearts and souls contributed to the formation and completion of this workbook. First and foremost, a deep bow to every person who has attended my Creative Discovery™ (initially called Creative Recovery™) workshops and retreats over the past fifteen years throughout the United States and at my weekly workshops at The Life Healing Center in Santa Fe, New Mexico. Thank you for trusting the creative process, and me, at one of the most vulnerable times in your life. Each one of you continues to inspire me more than you can ever imagine. Without you there would be no book to share.

Special thanks to my Emerald Flame Publishing team: treasured editor extraordinaire Mary Neighbour, who never fails to come in and make everything better, and to Michael Rohani at DesignForBooks.com for being full of creative ideas, talent, and a pleasure to work with. Thank you also to Page Lambert and Parvati Markus for your initial review and critique of the manuscript and to Grant Taylor for being a creative/technical genius and friend whom I am deeply grateful to.

Tremendous love, and gratitude go to Cynthia Rank-Ballas, my dear friend and sister who is always there for me, providing support, love, fun, inspiration and wisdom when I need it most.

I am lucky enough to have an incredible circle of friends/goddesses who graciously read early drafts of the manuscript and provided generous feedback in the form of encouragement, laughter, and suggestions to help make the book better: Jennifer Ferraro, Valerie Valentine, Eileen Hogan Grant, Anne Ribolow, Janet Ware, Christine Benjamin, Shelley Kinsella, Terri Wingham, Thea Witt, Lily Morrill and Sally Cush. How I respect, love, and adore each of you!

I also offer this in loving remembrance and praise of my two dear sisters Eliza Adams and Lexie Shabel who encouraged me, loved me, and cheered me on no matter what. They both died too young of metastatic breast cancer earlier this year. Their love of life and adventure are echoed in these pages and in the countless lives and hearts they touched with their selfless-service and presence. I am certain they are cheering us all on now.

Om Namah Shivaya to shining stars Jodie Varenya Franco and Antoine Yogesh Khoury for opening your home and hearts to me at a time when I needed it most. Your generosity and love provided a safe haven and creative nest for me to finish this book and start again. Forever grateful to you both and to Kathy Amba Christianson for being the best neighbors and friends I could wish for.

I have been fortunate to have had numerous teachers and mentors over the last twenty years, from many spiritual traditions and backgrounds, and I am grateful to each of them for sharing their wisdom and gifts, with me and many others. I won't name them all individually but must name: my parents, Freda Hanley, Joan Sutherland, Roshi, Rosvita Botkin PhD, Neem Karoli Baba and my beloved Amma. Thank you!

I place this at Her Lotus Feet.

About the Author

A passionate believer in the integration of body, mind, and spirit for living a full and joyful life, Pasha has been designing and leading Creative Discovery™ workshops for fifteen years across the globe.

Through her healing work and creative practices, she encourages people to stop believing everything they think they know about how life is supposed to go and instead start living from a place of wonder and curiosity, transforming fears into unknown possibilities.

That is the spiritual journey she embarked upon twenty years ago, when a third cancer diagnosis forced her to stop. She left behind the corporate world, trained as a psychotherapist, learned Reiki, discovered yoga and meditation, and began listening to the yearnings of her heart and soul.

Pasha collaborates with leading wellness organizations throughout the United States who share her interest in an integrative approach to healing and growth. Her work draws from personal experience, mytho-poetics, and ancient wisdom traditions from around the world. She designs her workshops and practices to serve as a transformative force, unlocking one's creative understanding, inherent wellbeing, and personal power.

Pasha loves living in the high desert of New Mexico, where she has a private healing practice, and also calls the islands of Maui and Ireland home.

If you would like Pasha to lead an innovative workshop or retreat or speak at your conference, please contact her at www.pashahogan.com.

Additional works by Pasha Hogan

"This book is a joy to read, and I could not put it down. Hogan is that rare author whose voice is so honest and clear that readers fall in love with her and cheer her on as she shares her journey in exquisite detail, warts and all, holding nothing back.

"Pasha writes so clearly, powerfully, and enchantingly... about the inherent creativity and triumphant spirit in everyone, waiting to be freed."

~ **LARRY DOSSEY, MD, author of *Reinventing Medicine* and *The Power of Premonitions***

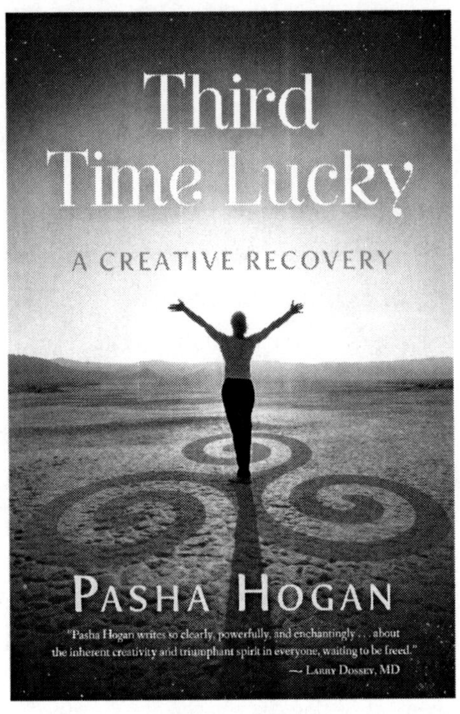

Please visit pashahogan.com for more information

Third Time Lucky: A Creative Recovery

Pasha Hogan's captivating story depicts how the devastating news of a third cancer diagnosis, at age thirty-one, catapults the author into the unknown territory of learning to love herself genuinely and honestly. It is the real-life account of a young woman's struggle and triumph over issues that affect every modern woman: sexuality, body image, empowerment and the journey toward truth. In Third Time Lucky, she invites readers to transform their own questions from, "Am I enough?" to "Am I enough of who I really am?"

Yoga: New Beginnings

DVD (68 min)

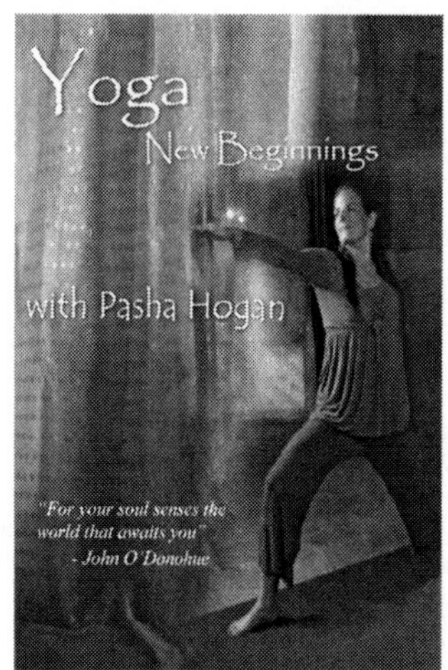

Join experienced yoga teacher Pasha Hogan on a guided journey of self-discovery, self-acceptance, and self-love. Learn to allow your breath to lead your way—instead of your thoughts—by following her morning and evening yoga practices demonstrated on this DVD. Pasha's style of teaching is inspirational and non-intimidating. Instructions are given in a clear and gentle way, welcoming absolute beginners and experienced practitioners alike. This is yoga in service of you!

Softening the Gaze

CD (70 min)

This CD offers two motivational talks and two meditations, inviting you into a kinder relationship with yourself and your inner critic. You learn to demystify your fears by getting to know and understand them, which enables you to take the next strides to a fuller life.

The Journey: No Detours

CD (73 min)

In this CD Pasha shares her personal experiences and insights as a three-time cancer survivor, inspiring you to lay down your burdens and follow your heart. It consists of three guided meditations, which you can use throughout your day. The ***Morning Meditation*** helps you start your day clear and centered, full of warmth and curiosity for new experiences. The Journey Meditation can be done at any time of day to help you lay down your burdens and relax more fully into life. The ***Evening Meditation*** assists you in moving into a restful and restorative sleep.

For more information and to purchase please visit
pashahogan.com

CPSIA information can be obtained
at www.ICGtesting.com
Printed in the USA
FFOW01n1902080318
45432255-46145FF